THREE WHO DARED

In the Same Series:

BONNIE
PONY OF THE SIOUX
THE JUNGLE SECRET
NORTH POLE: THE STORY OF
   ROBERT PEARY
BASEBALL BONUS KID
CAROL HEISS: OLYMPIC QUEEN
GREEN LIGHT FOR SANDY
SEA TREASURE
THE BLOOD RED BELT
KENDALL OF THE COAST GUARD
RODEO ROUNDUP
NANCY KIMBALL, NURSE'S AIDE
FOOTBALL FURY
CIVIL WAR SAILOR
DINNY AND DREAMDUST
AUSTIN OF THE AIR FORCE
THE LONG REACH
FOOTLIGHTS FOR JEAN
BASEBALL SPARK PLUG
RUNAWAY TEEN
LIGHTNING ON ICE
HOT ROD THUNDER
JUDY NORTH, DRUM MAJORETTE
DIRT TRACK DANGER
ADVENTURE IN ALASKA
CLIMB TO THE TOP
FISHING FLEET BOY
JACK WADE, FIGHTER FOR
   LIBERTY
THE MYSTERY OF HIDDEN
   HARBOR
SCANLON OF THE SUB SERVICE
A SUMMER TO REMEMBER
NAT DUNLAP, JUNIOR "MEDIC"
BLAST-OFF! A TEEN ROCKET
   ADVENTURE
TWO GIRLS IN NEW YORK
THE MYSTERY OF THE FLOODED
   MINE
CATHY AND LISETTE
EVANS OF THE ARMY
HIGH SCHOOL DROP OUT
DOUBLE TROUBLE
PRO FOOTBALL ROOKIE
THE MYSTERY OF BLUE STAR
   LODGE

ADVENTURE IN DEEPMORE CAVE
FAST BALL PITCHER
HI PACKETT, JUMPING CENTER
NURSE IN TRAINING
SHY GIRL: THE STORY OF
   ELEANOR ROOSEVELT
SKI PATROL
BIG BAND
GINNY HARRIS ON STAGE
GRACIE
THREE CHEERS FOR POLLY
SECOND YEAR NURSE
FEAR RIDES HIGH
THE MYSTERY OF THE INSIDE
   ROOM
ARTHUR ASHE: TENNIS CHAMPION
THE MYSTERY OF THE
   THIRD-HAND SHOP
GOING, GOING, GONE
THE KID FROM CUBA: ZOILO
   VERSALLES
GANG GIRL
TV DANCER
ROAR OF ENGINES
DONNA DEVARONA: GOLD MEDAL
   SWIMMER
PETE CASS: SCRAMBLER
BLACK SOLDIER
QUEEN OF ENGLAND: THE STORY
   OF ELIZABETH I
TROUBLE AT MERCY HOSPITAL
TRAPPED IN SPACE
MARTIN LUTHER KING: FIGHTER
   FOR FREEDOM
DANCE! THE STORY OF
   KATHERINE DUNHAM
THE TOMMY DAVIS STORY
FIRST LADY OF INDIA: THE
   STORY OF INDIRA GANDHI
RUNAWAY
SHIRLEY CHISHOLM
THREE WHO DARED
I WAS A BLACK PANTHER
THE TRUTH ABOUT DRUGS
MIGHTY HARD ROAD

THREE WHO DARED

By Tom Cohen

Doubleday & Company, Inc.
Garden City, New York

LIBRARY OF CONGRESS CATALOG CARD NUMBER 69–10998
COPYRIGHT © 1969 BY DOUBLEDAY & COMPANY, INC.
ALL RIGHTS RESERVED
PRINTED IN THE UNITED STATES OF AMERICA

PREPARED BY RUTLEDGE BOOKS

CONTENTS

ABOUT THIS BOOK

Until a few years ago, a Negro in the South had very few of the rights that most Americans—white Americans—have always taken for granted. Segregation laws, keeping whites and blacks apart, prevented Negroes from going to good schools and restaurants, forced them to sit in the back of public buses and ride in separate railroad cars, and kept them from using public rest rooms, parks, movie theaters, and even libraries. Very few good jobs were open to southern Negroes, and they often found it difficult or impossible to vote. Segregation was a way of life in the South and people in the rest of the country either ignored it or, if they opposed it, did nothing to end it.

Then, in the late 1950s and early 1960s a movement grew in the South to destroy segregation and win basic civil rights for the Negro. Young people of both races, first just a few, then by the thousands, joined together in a great struggle for justice and equality. Many gave up safe, comfortable lives in the North to join the movement and work in the southern states where the problems were the most serious. Some were beaten by angry whites, thrown in jail, chased by armed mobs; some were even murdered. But they all had a deep faith in the civil rights movement and were willing to give their lives for it.

As a result of their work, the South, in fact all of America, has changed. The movement made people all over the country understand the evils of segregation and race hatred. It forced the United States Government to enter the fight for civil rights by passing laws against segregation and giving protection to people working in the movement. It helped the Negro to gain the pride and dignity that for centuries whites had prevented him from attaining.

But a great many problems remain. The South has refused to obey many civil rights laws and the government has been slow to enforce them. Even whites who do obey the laws often still feel hatred for the Negro. And it has become clear that the race problem in the cities of the North is as serious as it is in the South.

But now the problems are out in the open where they can be struggled with and, someday, solved. The movement has changed greatly since it began, but it is still going on. And it will continue until all black Americans are given the rights, opportunities, and respect they deserve as citizens of this country.

This book tells the true stories of three young men—two of them white and one black—who had the courage to go south and help in this great fight for freedom.

THE
HENRY M. ARONSON
STORY

Chapter 1

THE GOOD LIFE

ANGER GROWS IN ALABAMA
AS DEMONSTRATIONS CONTINUE

Henry M. Aronson, 29 years old, with straight dark hair
and dark eyes, ignored the headline. He quickly skimmed
over the rest of the newspaper and then tossed it into
the waste basket. The poverty and suffering, war and
violence that filled the paper seemed far away as he sat
at his large, comfortable desk. It wasn't that the young
lawyer didn't care. He just didn't know much about the
problems of the world or even of his own country. And
anyway, what could *he* do about them? His main concern had always been with his own personal goals.

Now, in June 1964, he seemed to have found the
kind of life he wanted. As a lawyer in a large insurance company he was respected, well paid, and on

his way to becoming a success. Leaning back in his deep leather chair, his hands behind his head, Henry looked out of the window, high above the city of Hartford, Connecticut. Yes, he felt, for the first time in his life he was truly satisfied.

The ringing of his phone snapped Henry out of his pleasant thoughts. He answered and recognized the voice of his good friend Alan Levine in New York. Alan was always asking Henry to do the unexpected, like a ski trip to Colorado or a weekend in Paris. His voice certainly sounded excited enough now.

"How you doing, Henry?" his friend asked.

"Just great, Alan. Working hard. Living the good life. How's the big Wall Street lawyer?"

"Pretty good. I'm kind of bored, though. Not really enjoying my job. But I think I've found something that will be an interesting change."

Whatever it was, Henry was sure, it would be something out of the ordinary.

"What's that?"

"I'm going south with a group of civil rights lawyers to work with the Summer Project in Mississippi. Ever hear of it?"

Henry could not remember that he had. He knew nothing about the civil rights movement.

"Well," Alan explained, "hundreds of northern college students are spending the summer in the South helping Negroes exercise their right to vote, go to good schools, eat in any restaurants they want, and to use all public places. But they need lawyers. Without lawyers, they can't fight in the courts. Without lawyers, there's no way to get anything done."

"Go on," Henry said.

"I'm going down with the LCDC, the Lawyers' Constitutional Defense Committee. It's a group made up of lawyers who serve without pay—for two weeks. This is an important project, and I want to have a part in it. Why don't you come down too?"

"Why not?" Henry thought. It would be something different. It was a good cause. And, who knows, it might be fun.

"Sure, count me in," he said.

That afternoon he went to his boss and told him why he wanted two weeks off. To Henry's surprise, his boss thought it was a good idea. "If you think you can help, you should give it a try."

A week later, Henry Aronson was in Birmingham, Alabama. The LCDC had found enough lawyers for Mississippi, but they needed people in Alabama.

He went directly to where he had been told to report —a motel in the heart of the Negro district. It was something of a shock for Henry. He had known very few Negroes in his life and now he found himself in a completely black world. It made him feel uneasy. And the Negro section of a southern city is not a very pleasant place to live. But few of the public places in the city were integrated; that is, there were separate hotels for blacks and for whites. Only this Negro motel had opened its doors to both races. It had become the headquarters for civil rights work in the area and had been bombed several times by angry whites.

As Henry unpacked, a young white man dressed in slacks and a shirt appeared at the door. "Hi. I'm Bob Gorden. Okay if I come in?"

"Sure," Henry said, anxious to get to know someone.

"I'm one of the lawyers down here. After you get your things put away, let me take you around and show you how we operate."

"Thanks, that would be a big help," Henry answered. He looked beyond Bob and out to the front of the motel. People were driving in and out, others were just standing, looking stunned. "What's up?" Henry asked.

"Haven't you heard? Three civil rights workers—Andrew Goodman, Michael Schwerner, and James Chaney—disappeared last night. It seems pretty plain to us."

"Plain?"

"We think they've been murdered."

That night Henry realized that he was scared. He hadn't thought that working in the South could be that dangerous.

The next day, Henry received his first job. Several hundred Negro young men and women were being held in jail in Selma, Alabama, a town 75 miles to the south of Birmingham. Henry left right after breakfast.

His work there began much as he had expected, with a legal problem. Another lawyer, Ted Jackson, filled him in.

"Every day this week these people have been putting on demonstrations. They've been demanding their right to register to vote and calling for an end to the brutality of the sheriff and his cops.

"Every day the sheriff arrests them, and new ones take their places. So far he must have jailed hundreds. Now there's the problem of bail."

Bail was the amount of money you had to put up if you were in jail and wanted to be released until the day of your trial.

"The local judge has set such high bail that it is impossible to raise enough money," Ted explained. "Unless we do something, those people can be kept in jail for months."

Henry had an idea. "You know the Supreme Court decision about bail having to be fair? It said that bail can be only high enough to make sure the person appears when his trial is held."

"So?" Ted said.

"Well, as you know, these town courts have to obey decisions made by federal courts. If we get statements from each of the kids in jail proving that they have little or no money, we can go to federal court and prove that the bails are too high. Then the court can order that bail be set lower."

A few hours later, Henry walked up the steps of the county jail with statements for the prisoners to sign. He asked politely to be taken to their cells. The man in charge gave Henry a look that was ugly with hatred.

When Henry saw the cells, he couldn't believe it. In each, ten young Negroes were packed into space for four. They had no beds, no mattresses, no showers, or toilets. Outside, the thermometer stood at 100 degrees.

Henry went from cell to cell, speaking to each man in turn, showing how to fill out the statements. Before long he forgot the heat. He was impressed by the prisoners' spirit and courage.

Henry was getting his first close-up look at the treatment of Negroes in the South, and he didn't like what he saw. Perhaps for the first time in his life, he found himself deeply interested in somebody other than Henry Aronson.

It was late in the afternoon when he left the jail house. His next job was to get to the sheriff and give him the legal papers that would force him into court himself. The catch was, he had to be served in person. Henry would have to find a way to get directly to the sheriff.

It would have been a simple task in the North, but in Selma it was a difficult and possibly dangerous mission. Many people were trying to serve the sheriff papers, so he was in hiding. And because of his hatred of civil rights workers there was no telling what he would do if he met one face to face.

Henry went to the county court house. From the entrance he could see the sheriff's office at the far end of a long hall filled with people. How could he get through without being stopped?

Holding the papers firmly and taking a deep breath, Henry walked boldly through the entrance into the hall. With the loudest, most southern accent he could manage, he said, "Hi! How ya doin'?" to the first person he met.

"Why, fine," was the pleased answer.

No one stopped him, so he kept working his way down the hall smiling and saluting everyone with a loud, friendly greeting until he found himself in front of the sheriff's office. Without pausing, he walked right in.

A secretary looked up from her desk. Henry was wearing a big, dumb grin. "Hi. Jim in?" he asked.

The secretary smiled back at him. "Just a minute, let me see." She went to the door of an inside office, opened it, and spoke to someone. A second later, the huge, 220-pound sheriff walked out.

With a smile, Henry reached out and put the legal notice in the sheriff's hands. "Sheriff, you're served."

The color drained from the sheriff's face. His mouth open, he stared first at Henry, then at the paper in his hand. Henry turned on his heels and walked quickly out the door. Behind him he could hear the secretary almost in tears, saying over and over, "I'm sorry, Jim. I'm sorry. He acted like he was a friend."

Later in the day, Henry and his fellow lawyers presented their case before the U.S. district judge. The judge ruled in their favor. He ordered the local court to lower the bail to a sum the Negroes could pay.

As they filed out of the court room, Henry passed the sheriff. He thought he heard the man say, "He better watch out if he knows what's good for him."

Henry thought nothing of it—he still had a lot to learn about the risks he was taking.

Henry hurried back to the jail to see that the young men were released.

"You sure worked fast," one of them said.

"You really must know what you are doing," said another.

Henry felt a sense of pride he had never known before. He had been able to employ his training and talent to work for several hundred human beings who had no one else to turn to. It gave him a satisfaction that no business success had ever given him.

But there was still much to do in the two weeks he would be in the South.

He went to the jail's front office, where he saw the man in charge sitting at his desk.

"May I use your phone?" Henry asked him pleasantly.

To his surprise, the man answered in a friendly manner. "Sure thing. Why don't you use the one on the wall over there?"

Henry thanked him and started to make the call.

Just then the sheriff walked into the room. He looked at Henry for a moment, then spoke in low tones to the man at the desk. Finally, he walked over to Henry and bellowed, "Who the hell told you you could use my phone?"

Before Henry could answer, the sheriff grabbed him by the arms, lifted him off the ground, and threw him against the wall. Henry fell to the floor. The sheriff picked him up as if he were a rubber ball and bounced him off the wall again. Then he threw him, bruised and frightened, the length of the hall. Giving Henry a final shove into the elevator, the sheriff yelled, "Now you get the hell out of my jail and don't come back again!"

Henry picked himself up off the floor. He was badly shaken. The physical pain wasn't so bad. It was the knowledge that this could happen—to him—here in America. He lay awake that night thinking about it. His body ached. And he could still see the faces of the Negroes, packed in their hot cells. The next day, as Henry left Selma, he knew one thing for sure. The bruises would heal and the fear would disappear, but he would never forget this day. He would never forget what had happened to him. In fact, nothing in his life would ever be the same again.

Chapter 2

"I CAN'T JUST LEAVE"

Henry stared out of the window of his Birmingham motel room. The Negro neighborhood and the black faces, which had seemed so strange and frightening when he had first arrived, now had a familiar almost comforting look. Time had passed so quickly since he had come south, it was hard to believe that his two weeks were up. He had been working on civil rights cases from all over Alabama. Many people needed help and there were very few lawyers to help them. Although the work was hard and tiring and often ended in failure, it was the most important and worth-while work Henry had ever done in his life.

Now that his time was up, Henry had to decide what to do next. A lot had happened and he had done many things he could be proud of. But there was still so much to be done. He called his boss in Hartford and spoke to him at length. Ten minutes after he hung up he heard a knock on the door. It was one of the LCDC leaders.

He looked worried. "I have something I want to discuss with you, Henry," he began. "We've got 6 lawyers over in Mississippi. Now that their two weeks are up, they're all heading back north and a new batch is coming down. We need someone with experience to be in charge of their work. We've just opened an office in Memphis, Tennessee, on the Mississippi border, to handle all civil rights cases in the northern area of Mississippi. How would you like to run that office?"

"Thanks," Henry said, "but do you think I've had enough experience?"

"Henry, as civil rights lawyers go, you're an old pro." Then he frowned. "Is there any chance I can talk you into staying?"

"No problem. I just spoke to my boss. The company has agreed to give me another month."

Henry moved to Memphis and took charge of the LCDC office. There were always too many cases and not enough people to handle them. Henry worked furiously, getting more involved in the movement every day. Most of his work consisted of getting people out of jail and bringing legal action against restaurants, theaters, or even local governments, that refused to give Negroes their rights.

Toward the end of the month, an adviser to COFO

(Council of Federated Organizations), which planned most of the civil rights activities in Mississippi, came to see Henry, to ask him to become COFO's head lawyer.

Henry faced an important decision. The problems were enormous and the material rewards were small. He'd be paid half as much as he was making at the insurance company. And the hours he'd be working would be twice as long. He'd have many nights without sleep and a good share of danger. It took him no time at all, however, to reach a decision. The next day he flew back to the headquarters of his company in Hartford.

"I've come back," Henry said to his boss, "to explain in person my reasons for resigning. Now that I'm here I find it hard to put what I feel into words. I just know I can't leave the South now. All summer long we've been telling the Negroes what their rights are and encouraging them to fight for those rights. Now all the white kids are going back to college, and the lawyers are checking out too. I can't just pack up and leave. There's such a tremendous need. There are only three Negro lawyers in the entire state and there isn't a single white lawyer from Mississippi willing to handle civil rights cases. There are almost a million black people in Mississippi and many of them need help desperately. I want to stay and do whatever I can."

If Henry had expected his boss not to understand, he was wrong. The older man smiled warmly. "There are few times in a man's life that he has an opportunity to do something in which he really believes. You're very lucky. We'd like you to stay with us, but it's clear to me that you're doing the right thing. I wish you the best of luck."

The next four months were hard ones for the movement and for Henry. He worked out of a tiny office in Jackson, Mississippi, with one secretary and a part time assistant. A great mass of cases had piled up on his desk. He couldn't handle them all himself, so he had to find lawyers in other organizations who would be willing to represent the people involved.

Then, to his dismay, Henry discovered that COFO was breaking up. Too many white civil rights workers were returning to the North. There was no money. COFO could not afford to pay his salary. Henry had been living off his savings. Soon he was also paying for part of the office expenses. When he came to the end of his savings, he borrowed money and kept on going. At the end of the year, COFO ceased operations altogether.

Henry was discouraged, but he had no intention of giving up. He wasn't going to leave the South. In January, the Legal Defense Fund of the National Association for the Advancement of Colored People hired him to work with two other lawyers in their Jackson office.

There, in addition to getting people out of jail and desegregating hotels and restaurants, Henry and the other lawyers provided legal aid to Negroes who tried to enter all white schools. He had been surprised to learn that most school districts spent only half to a quarter as much money on black pupils as they did on whites. Armed with these facts, he prepared case after case.

Henry continued to work for the Legal Defense Fund throughout 1965 and into the following year. He traveled all over the state, meeting with the parents and children involved in every case. He often went to the white schools with Negro children on their first day. He attended community meetings, visited men in their cells, pleaded his cases in court.

There always seemed to be too many people asking for help. The lawyers were always behind, always working around the clock. But Henry just couldn't turn anybody down. He felt he had a duty to every one who came to him. He felt that if you told people about their rights, you owed it to them to be there to back them up when they put into practice what they had been told.

There were many times when he suffered a sense of despair. He felt unable to bring about a real change to end the fear and misery of the black people.

Early in June, Henry traveled to Washington, D.C. He sat in his hotel room, listening to the radio, enjoying a rare moment of rest, far from the pressures of the South. Suddenly he straightened up in his chair.

But a news man interrupted the music. "James Meredith was shot late this afternoon on the first day of his march through Mississippi."

Henry reached over and turned up the radio.

"Meredith, who gained attention all over the world when he became the first Negro to enter the University of Mississippi in 1962, set out earlier today with a handful of people to walk from the Tennessee border to Jackson, Mississippi, on his March Against Fear. His aim was to prove to the Negroes of that state that they could exercise their rights without fear of attack. He had walked only ten miles when he was shot in the head by a shotgun blast fired from a wooded area at the side of the road in the small town of Hernando, Mississippi. Civil rights leaders, who had not paid much attention to Meredith's march before the shooting, are rushing to the scene. First reports said that the 33-year-old Negro had been killed. However, the latest word is that he is alive, but in very serious condition."

Henry jumped up immediately and called his office. In five minutes he was packed, out the door, and on his way to Memphis.

Chapter 3

MARCH AGAINST FEAR

The Meredith shooting shocked the nation. Hundreds of men and women poured into Memphis to finish James Meredith's march. For two days civil rights people, including Henry, worked on plans for organizing the marchers. Then the marchers gathered at Hernando, Mississippi, the tiny town which had become the center of national attention. There they began their 180-mile sweep south through the center of the state.

Dozens of news men and TV crews were covering the event. FBI men mixed in with the marchers, while State Highway Patrol men went ahead to check for bombs on every bridge and underpass in the marchers' path.

Henry returned to his office in Jackson. Every evening he drove to where the marchers were stopping for the night to be available in case of trouble and to give his legal services to Martin Luther King, Jr., and the other leaders.

Hour after hour they walked in the hot summer sun. Blacks and whites marched side by side past great plantations. Freedom songs drifted over the cotton fields where dark stooping figures worked much as they had in slave days. The Highway Patrol men, so often accused of keeping power through force and terror, were now guarding a group of blacks and whites who were trying to change the very society the police had promised to protect. The news men, secretly hoping for that "big story" of violence, by their very presence prevented it. Local officials in towns along the way were helping register Negroes who would probably vote them out of office. It was beautiful. It was too good to last.

The first hint of trouble came when the marchers had gone about 75 miles and reached Grenada. In spite of all the laws and the Supreme Court decisions, there wasn't a school, restaurant, gas station, or public pool that was integrated in Grenada.

However, city officials, hoping to avoid incidents, had bowed to the leaders' wishes, so that the marchers could pass through with little trouble. They changed their age-old system of making it almost impossible for Negroes to register to vote. They hired six Negro clerks in the voting office and agreed to keep it open at night so Negroes could register after work.

That day 300 Negroes in Grenada registered to vote.

Henry was pleased, but he knew it was too early to celebrate. The anger of the whites was building swiftly.

Henry heard the word going around that Grenada had "sold out" to the civil rights leaders. City officials were being accused of giving in. Hour by hour, the pressure mounted. When the marchers were 20 miles down the road, the Grenada town officials acted. They closed the registration office, fired the Negro clerks, and went back on their promises. When the news reached the marchers, Dr. King was furious.

"They have not seen the last of us," Dr. King said. "We will be back."

The march proceeded without incident until it was within 25 miles of Jackson. Suddenly the violence that everyone feared broke out. The marchers had decided to camp that night on the grounds of the Negro high school. No sooner had they set up their tents than city officials ordered them off the field. They refused to go, and the Highway Patrol opened fire on them with tear gas, driving them half-blind and choking off the school grounds. Later, the leaders gathered to draw up a statement on the attack.

"What's our legal position on this?" Dr. King asked Henry.

Henry thought long and hard. "I'm afraid your rights aren't very clear in this case," he said at last. "The school is city property, and the city probably has the right to keep you off it." Henry sensed how disappointed the men around him were. Many of them were anxious to make a strong protest anyway, but Dr. King held them back. He spoke slowly and with a trace of sadness.

"I've been on a great many civil rights demonstrations and always, not only the moral right but the *law* has been on my side. Those are the only truly strong demonstrations. From what you have told me, I don't feel this demonstration is really strong. When we speak to the nation we must have the law on our side. The nation doesn't understand moral rights unless they are backed up by legal rights. So I urge you not to fight too hard on this issue."

Two days later the marchers reached the state capitol in Jackson. There they gathered for a final mass meeting. James Meredith was sufficiently recovered from his wounds to address the happy crowds. The 15-day March Against Fear was declared a success.

But Martin Luther King, Jr., had not forgotten Grenada's actions. At the end of the meeting, he announced that he was sending back half a dozen civil rights workers to Grenada. They had instructions to organize a movement there. Henry felt a sense of relief now that the march was over. He had no way of knowing that the results would soon involve him in his most dangerous role in the civil rights movement.

Chapter 4

GRENADA

Saturday afternoon, a few days later, Henry was working in his Jackson office when the phone rang. It was one of the civil rights workers who had returned to Grenada.

"We held our first demonstration in Grenada today," he announced. "When the police moved in, they arrested 20 guys. Can you help us get them out of jail?"

"Sure," Henry assured him. "What kind of fight is the city putting up?"

"They're acting pretty rough. They gave in to us during the march but I don't think they're ever going to do that again."

"I can get to work on it right away," said Henry. "Don't worry."

Henry made some phone calls and then went to Grenada, where he talked to the county attorney and got the

20 men released from jail. Thinking there would be no more trouble, he returned to Jackson that night.

Two days later the SCLC (Southern Christian Leadership Conference) workers in Grenada tried to organize a large group at a Fourth of July picnic on a Negro owned farm. Immediately, they were arrested and jailed. Henry rushed back to Grenada. After getting the release on bail of a few of the leaders, he returned to his office to prepare papers for their trial.

The national press recognized that an important story was in the making. News men started moving into the Mississippi city. All that was necessary to set off a real movement was something to stir the bottled-up anger of Grenada's black citizens.

On July 10, it came. A large group staged a protest march to the jail. They were met by the Mississippi Highway Patrol who attacked them, swinging clubs and firing tear gas. A Negro wandered over to see what was happening. The police ordered him to move on. He started to leave, but the police didn't think he moved fast enough. Ten Highway Patrol men surrounded him. Then, in full view of everybody, one of the policemen beat him to the ground. The incident was well covered by film crews and later that night was shown to the nation on TV. The local Negroes who had "stayed in their place" for centuries were shaken and angered. The time had come to act.

The next day Henry moved to Grenada to be at the

center of things. He and another worker set up a "branch office" of the Legal Defense Fund in the Monte Cristo Motel. They were not alone. The FBI arrived in force at the motel. They began putting up sending and receiving radio sets. The Mississippi Highway Patrol took over a few rooms as a command post and also put in radios. Other rooms were filled with people from the Justice Department in Washington, government lawyers, and news men.

A 24-year-old law student came down to join Henry's group. His name was Ollie Rosengard. He was filled with fresh, eager enthusiasm.

On Ollie's first evening there they were having dinner together in the motel dining room. Ollie hardly touched his meal. He was too busy looking around him.

"Who are all these guys?"

Henry started pointing them out—workers with the movement, FBI men, government agents, reporters—all watching each other, listening, waiting.

"It's quite a cast of characters," Ollie said. Then he returned to the business at hand. "Has the movement been making any progress?"

"The whites haven't given an inch. They say they'd rather go out of business than give in. We've been suing everyone in sight—the movie house, the swimming pool, four restaurants, the school superintendent, the Mississippi Highway Patrol, the county and city authorities. The suits will take a long time. But we have been able legally to force the state and local police to provide protection for the marchers. So far they've been doing it. All we have to do is give the authorities an hour's notice when we are going to march. Then they're bound by law to protect us."

Henry looked at his watch. "We had better get going. The march is starting in a few minutes." He stood up and then motioned toward the other tables with a smile. "Look at this." All around them people were looking at their watches, calling for their checks, and streaming from the room.

When they reached the town square, it was surrounded by over 500 whites. A ring of 150 Highway Patrol men kept the square clear for the marchers. In the crowd were a number of white boys and girls wearing Louisiana State University and University of Mississippi T-shirts. They were laughing and chattering.

"They act like it's a football game," Ollie said to Henry with surprise.

"Yes," said Henry. "It's the biggest sport in Mississippi. They come from miles around and bring their dates to 'see the niggers march.' Then there's the type that comes to 'get the niggers.' Some of them are in the Ku Klux Klan and many of them bring their guns."

Ollie looked around and saw groups of tough-looking farmers standing about. Anger was in their faces. Some of them had heavy sticks, large slingshots, or hunting rifles.

Then, above the noise, the sound of singing could be heard, getting louder and louder as the marchers approached.

>*We shall overcome.*
>*We shall overcome.*
>*We shall overcome some day. . . .*

A thousand black men and women—young people and grand parents—people the whites had only seen picking cotton, pushing a broom, taking out garbage, or shining shoes—marched proudly into the town square with their heads high, singing at the top of their voices.

>*Deep in our hearts*
>*We do believe*
>*We shall overcome some day.*

"I can't believe it," Ollie whispered to Henry.

Henry nodded. "Last week there were only about a hundred."

The marchers assembled in the square, and one of the SCLC leaders began to speak. From the circle of whites came cries of, "Burn the niggers. Let's get them. Kill them! Kill the dirty niggers!" Large steel balls fired from slingshots buzzed like giant bees, disappearing among the marchers.

But the demonstrators showed no fear. The leader spoke with strength and courage. He talked about violent cops, crooked city officials, and all the whites who had denied the Negroes their rights. He put into words all the feelings of anger that black people had kept inside them throughout their lives. They had always been alone and powerless. Now they were united in a great cause. They cheered the speaker's words and stood up to the mob. They weren't begging for favors from the whites. They were demanding their rights.

When the demonstration ended, Ollie said, "I hate to admit it, Henry, but I was scared."

"I'd like to say that you'll get used to it, but I never have. I just get more and more scared. The hate in that white mob can't be held back forever. One of these days it's going to cut loose and when it does . . . I don't even want to think about it.

"And another cheery thing to keep in mind. Only a few of us working with the movement here are white. The more people get to know who we are—get to know our faces—the more dangerous it's going to be. I already feel as if there's a big sign over me that says civil rights worker."

Henry noticed that Ollie had turned pale. "Well, maybe it's not quite that bad," Henry added. "But, just the same, be careful."

Chapter 5

THE BOILING POINT

The demonstrations continued well into July. Emotions were reaching the boiling point. There was more violence. More people were injured. Forty or fifty more Negroes were arrested. The city jail bulged with more prisoners than it could handle. The cells were over crowded and the food was terrible. Henry got permission to visit the kids every day and take them food.

One evening Henry sent Ollie on ahead to one of the Negro churches to pick up some food for the prisoners. When Henry was ready to leave for the church, Jim Draper, a friend of Henry's from the Justice Department in Washington, offered to give Henry a ride.

Everything was quiet when they reached the church. Ollie's car was parked in front, but it was empty. Even the building looked empty. Henry sensed that something was wrong. They pulled up behind Ollie's car and got out to look around. The only sound to be heard was a frog croaking in the distance. The street was dark. A figure came slowly out of the bushes. It was Ollie. They met him at the back of their car.

"What happened?" Henry asked, his voice shattering the quiet. Ollie put his finger to his lips.

"Shh. When I got here, two white guys were standing next to the church," Ollie whispered, looking around nervously. "They asked me what I was doing and I told them I was just getting some food. I went in. I should have ducked right out the back or called the cops. Like a fool, I didn't. I got the food and went back out and started to put it in the car. The guys were still there. One of them pulled out a gun and told me to get going."

"Where are they now?" asked Henry. Ollie don't answer. He was looking over toward the church. Henry turned quickly. Two men were standing in the shadows. One of them was holding a machine gun!

"Quick," Henry whispered, "get under the car." The three of them dived under the car and lay there without moving. They could hear foot steps coming closer. Then a voice grunted, "Shoot! Shoot!"

"Let's get out of here," Henry said. They crawled out from under the car and started running down the street. Behind them the gun was being fired in short bursts. Henry heard bullets flying past his head.

The three dashed around the corner, ran up to a house,

and dived under it, crawling back away from the street. They lay there trying to breathe quietly, their hearts pounding.

Henry looked at Draper. The older man had kept up with them the whole way. "Boy, Jim, you sure can run," he said between deep breaths.

"Maybe that's why they gave me this job," Draper said with a slight smile.

"Oh no," Ollie whispered, "here they come again!"

A car screamed to a halt outside the house. After a moment it sped off. A minute later it rounded the corner with tires squealing and raced past the house once more. It drove around the block again and then disappeared.

When it seemed safe, they crawled out and stood up. Henry ran into the corner house and asked if he could use the phone to call the chief of police.

"You almost had three murders on your hands," Henry said when the chief answered. He then went on to tell in detail what had just happened.

"You just sit tight, Henry. We'll be right over," the chief said, and hung up.

Minutes later, several police and Highway Patrol cars arrived at the scene. The chief was there with the sheriff and several Highway Patrol men.

Ollie gave them a description of the men with the gun and a call went out on the police radio to arrest them. A message came back saying they had just been picked up. They had pulled a gun on a white woman and tried to hold up a store owned by the uncle of one of the town's policemen! The chief gave instructions to book the two men for attempted murder.

A few days later, the men were released. "I guess people don't consider it a crime to shoot a civil rights worker in Grenada, any more," Henry thought when he was told the news.

Then, on the Saturday night following the shooting, Henry heard that a thousand armed whites had gathered in the town square and were waiting for the marchers to arrive. He got in his car and drove slowly around the square. The place was filled with whites, openly carrying rifles, pistols, clubs, and slingshots. Dozens of tough dirt farmers driving pick-up trucks with rifle racks up against the back windows raced around and around, hooting and yelling. It had all the spirit of a good old-fashioned hoe down—and all the makings of a blood bath.

Henry drove directly to the church. He was almost late, for the marchers were already assembling. He could hear the voices of 300 Negroes singing freedom songs inside. They were eager to march and unafraid of what might happen to them. Henry hurried to a room in the back of the church. There ten leaders of the Grenada movement were trying to decide whether or not to march. Henry spoke up quickly.

"I just had a look downtown," he said. "I suggest you call off the demonstration. It's much too dangerous."

"If we give in to the mob now, the movement will fall apart," protested one of the leaders.

"We have to take that chance," another put in. "If our people get too scared, they'll never march again."

"They'll have to learn to face their fear," said still another. "We've got to march."

Henry heard a loud noise outside. He went to the window and looked out. Highway Patrol cars had surrounded the church. On their roofs stood state police wearing gas masks to protect themselves against tear gas. Rifles with fixed bayonets were in their hands. In the distance Henry could hear rebel yells.

"The mob got tired of waiting. They're coming to storm the church!" he cried. Then Henry saw the sheriff and a county officer outside. He rushed out to talk to them.

"Please, Henry, tell them to call it off," pleaded the officer when he saw the young lawyer.

"I can't hold those white folks back any longer," said the sheriff. "You gotta tell your people not to march."

Inspector Glenn of the Highway Patrol came running over. "We got them moving in another direction," he said quickly. "But they'll be back. We can't handle them. We've only got 360 highway police in the whole state and 300 of them are here tonight."

"I can't very well tell them what to do," Henry said, "but I can pass on your advice." Henry went back into the church.

He explained the situation to the leaders. After more argument, they finally agreed to call off the march. Henry went back outside to inform the police officials. "The march is being called off," he said, "but we must have your protection for our people on their way home."

The police officials talked it over. A few minutes later a patrol man brought him the reply. "Sorry. We can't guarantee their protection."

Now Henry was really alarmed. "How are we going to get 300 black people safely to their homes with a white mob roaming around looking for blood?" he protested. Then he had an idea.

He ran to a patrol car and called Inspector Glenn on its radio. He tried to sound calm.

"Inspector, this is Henry Aronson. I'm giving you one hour's notice. We are marching tonight after all. We demand protection!"

Before Glenn could reply, Henry turned and walked away.

"Now all we have to do is lay out a route that goes past everyone's house." Henry smiled to himself. "Then we'll just march them all home!"

Three minutes later several police cars drew up in front of the church. Inspector Glenn and the sheriff got out of their cars and rushed over to him.

"Henry," said the sheriff, "don't do this to me. Call off the march, will you?"

The inspector looked worried. "Look, I tell you what.

I've got 94 patrol cars. Suppose I get my men to give everyone a ride home. How about that?"

"Well," said Henry, "let me pass your offer along to the leaders, and see what they say."

Inside the church, he described the plan.

"Absolutely not," a SCLC worker insisted. "I'm not letting those cops drive anyone home in those cars. It'll scare them so that they'll never march again."

It looked like an impossible situation when suddenly someone stuck his head in the door from the main hall of the church.

"Everything's all right!" called the man with a broad grin. "Seems the mob heard that we were going to march, so they all went back to the square to get ready for us. Soon as they were gone, our people started slipping home by themselves."

Henry saw through the door that the church was already half empty and Negroes were flooding out into the street. "I hope I don't have to go through many more nights like this."

"Let's not just sit here," said one of the SCLC leaders. "We had better start planning tomorrow's demonstration."

Chapter 6

"SEE YOU IN COURT!"

All through August the white citizens of Grenada looked on while the Negro movement grew larger and stronger. Fall was near, and with it the opening of school. Civil rights leaders began a major effort to sign up Negro children for the white school. With new pride and courage, the Negro community enrolled 300 children in the white high school. School officials had no choice but to accept them. The police were called upon to see that no one caused trouble. It looked as though the movement had won a major victory.

About a week before school opened, Henry was transferred to the Legal Defense Fund's New York office to work on school law suits throughout the South. He had mixed feelings about leaving as he had been with the Grenada movement since its birth. All around him he could still see much to be done. And yet, in New York he would be handling school cases not just for one city but for hundreds all over the South. And both the Highway Patrol and the Justice Department had assured him that the Negro children would be protected by the police when they entered the white school on September 9.

Shortly before school was to open, Henry left Mississippi and started driving north. He was coming over the bridge to Washington, D.C., listening to the news on his car radio, when he heard:

"In Grenada, Mississippi, today, when Negro school children arrived at the formerly all white high school and tried to enter, they were attacked by a mob of over a thousand screaming whites. The children were beaten with clubs and chains and many had to be taken to the hospital." News men also were badly beaten; cameras were smashed; and automobiles destroyed. Only a handful of the Mississippi Highway Patrol and local police, who had kept order in Grenada throughout a summer of civil rights demonstrations, were present at the scene, and they made no effort to prevent the mob's actions. One man called it the ugliest school opening in history.

Henry was shocked. The New York job would have to wait. He drove directly to the air port and caught the next plane south. In Grenada, Henry went right to work. Throughout the night he and his associates drew up legal papers, met with police, and spoke with a district judge.

The Mississippi Highway Patrol called in every man

it had from all over the state to protect the children. The local police promised that the violence of the first day would not be repeated.

At 7:30 in the morning Henry got up and drove over to the school. He wanted to see if everything was all right before the opening. He stepped out of his car to look around. The Highway Patrol was not in sight, but since the plan was to keep them hidden to avoid causing any violence, Henry wasn't surprised. In front of the school stood a county police official.

Then Henry saw five men standing in a parking lot near the school. In their hands they held tire irons and heavy chains. The officer glanced in their direction and then nodded his head toward the young lawyer. The five men rushed at Henry the second the officer made the gesture. Henry ran toward the officer. The five men caught him first and knocked him to the ground. They began hitting him with their chains and irons. Henry crawled on his knees and managed to get his hands on the police officer's feet. "Help me, help me," he pleaded.

The officer stood silent and watched. A single thought ran through Henry's mind. "They're going to kill me. If he won't save me, nobody's going to save me."

Then an ABC TV camera unit moved in and began to record the incident on film. When Henry's attackers saw the cameras, they stalked silently away.

Henry lay still at the officer's feet, badly bruised and in a state of shock.

"What the hell are you doing here?" the officer asked, glaring down at him, not helping him to get up.

"I came to see if everything was taken care of," Henry answered, trying to get to his feet.

Roughly the officer helped Henry stand up.

"Now get out of here before anything worse happens to you," he ordered. "I hope you've learned your lesson."

Henry sat for a few moments behind the wheel of his car, waiting for his head to clear. Then he started the engine and slowly drove away.

Catching a look at himself in the rear view mirror, Henry was startled at the sight of his battered face and frightened eyes. Suddenly all the feelings of disappointment and anger that had built up within him over the past few months poured out in a flood of thoughts.

"A lot of good the law did me today. I was helpless." Although he had always hated violence, now he had pictures in his mind of smashing his five attackers with a few well aimed punches. "I wish I had a gun," he thought. "That would have stopped them." He saw himself coolly holding them at gun point and then marching them off to jail. "Violence is the only thing they understand. Everything else is a waste of time."

He saw a car behind him in the rear view mirror. "Somebody's following me," he thought. His fear grew as the car stayed close behind him for two more blocks. Then it turned a corner and disappeared. Henry sank back in the seat with relief. He knew the effects of the beating would last long after his bruises healed. He'd be afraid to drive at night. And he'd always think he was being followed, always live in fear of an ambush.

"If I feel this way, what about all those kids? After what they've been through, they'll never last in that white school. They'll start dropping out until only a few of the bravest are left." That thought released all the hidden doubts he had about his work in the movement.

"They'll never be able to keep the demonstrations going—the city will keep the swimming pool closed rather than desegregate it—we'll integrate a few restaurants but no Negroes will be able to afford eating in them—even if we send a few crooked officials to jail, others will come and take their places—there will be endless cases and long delays in getting them to trial—no big changes—when the Negroes see that everything has stayed the same, why should they go on risking their necks—they'll lose interest—the leaders will move on to another town—and the movement will slow down and then die."

In this moment of pain and anger, Henry wiped from his mind all that he had worked so hard for. His thoughts went back to a day two years earlier. He was sitting in his safe, comfortable office doing his well paid job for the insurance company. Why had he ever left?

The sight of a policeman standing on a street corner suddenly forced a more recent memory into Henry's mind. He saw the police official standing in front of the school with his fists on his hips ordering Henry to leave. "I hope you've learned your lesson," he could hear the officer say.

Henry's mood suddenly changed. He spoke to the imagined police officer defiantly. "You'd like it if I gave up, wouldn't you?" Now he remembered why he was in the South. It was because of officers like him and the brutal sheriffs with their violent cops and the mobs with their chains and shotguns. It was because the fear he was now experiencing was part of the everyday life of millions of black people. They needed his help and he had to give it. Whether in Grenada or New York, he'd keep on helping. He'd fight the small battles and hope they'd grow into big ones. If one method failed, he'd try another. No, he wouldn't quit, and neither would Grenada's black people. This movement might end, because it grew too fast and depended too much on outside leaders. But people had stood up to worse beatings than Henry's and they had come back night after night —they wouldn't give up.

Henry stopped in front of the motel. He had a lot of work to do and a lot to tell the judge. He kept the police official's image in his mind for a moment longer.

"I may not carry a gun or be able to match you with violence," he thought, "but I've got my own legal weapons."

Henry got out of the car and let the image fade from his mind.

"So long for now, *friend*. I'll see you in court!"

THE
JOHN O'NEAL
STORY

Chapter 1

THE GROWING YEARS

John O'Neal stood at the edge of the outdoor stage waiting to go on. Flickering shadows played over the young Negro's face. Swarms of insects danced around flood light bulbs stuck in large tomato cans. Blinking, he looked beyond the glare of the lights into the damp Mississippi night. A hundred black faces stared toward the stage. They were young people in their teens and old men and women. Many had never been to school; none had ever seen a play. They stood or sat on benches in the parking lot of the McComb Freedom House.

Just two years earlier, John's greatest dream had been to live in New York and write plays. What had happened to that dream? Why was he 1300 miles from New York City on this hot summer night in July 1964?

John had grown up in Mound City, Illinois, a tiny

town in the southern tip of the state where the Mississippi and Ohio rivers meet. Bordered by the states of Missouri and Kentucky, the 2000 people in Mound City lived by the traditions of the South. For half the population, Mound City's Negroes, that meant segregation.

John grew up completely apart from whites, living in an all black community, playing only with Negro children, going to an all black school and church.

His parents, both teachers, raised him and his younger brother and sister with warmth and intelligence. He never had the feeling that there was anything *wrong* with being black. It was obvious to him that it was the system that was wrong, not him. But he didn't think much about the problems of his race. He was just a kid and had more pleasant things to concern himself with. Anyway, in those days people weren't doing much about segregation. It was just a fact of life.

When John was about to enter high school in 1954, he read in the papers that the Supreme Court had ruled segregation in the public schools was contrary to the Constitution. John and his friends were very excited.

"Now we can have a great basketball team!" John had exclaimed. "There'll be all those white kids to draw from."

He also believed that he would be getting a better education, since his parents had told him that the Negro schools were not as good as the white schools.

On the first day of school he was surprised and disappointed to see that the school was just as it always had been. All the students were black. He wasn't bitter or angry, just annoyed at the stupidity of it. That night he wrote a letter to the state superintendent of education.

"It was my understanding," he wrote, "that the Supreme Court decision of last May made it against the law to operate segregated schools, and I am still going to a segregated school. I just wondered if your office knew this and what you plan to do about it."

John never received an answer to his letter.

He was especially upset by the way his parents felt about the Supreme Court decision. They, like so many other Negro teachers, were afraid that they would lose their jobs to whites if the schools were integrated. According to everything they had taught John, they should have been *for* integration. And yet they seemed to be frightened by it.

John had always been disturbed that people didn't always act according to their beliefs. He took his own religious beliefs very seriously. Sunday school had been an important part of his life.

John felt that religion taught you how to live every day, not just on Sunday. Yet all around him people would say one thing and then do the opposite. Now his parents were doing the same thing with integration.

He was approaching the draft age and he saw that he would soon have to face a conflict between what he had always been taught as a child and what he would be told as an older person. Fighting, he had been taught, is bad; violence doesn't solve anything. The Bible said: "Thou shalt not kill." Now, as an adult, he would be told he must join the Army, he must fight, he must kill. It was a problem he knew he'd have to face some day.

After finishing high school in three years, John entered Southern Illinois University at Carbondale, 60 miles to the north of his home. It was his first real contact with whites. He was worried that he would have trouble, having gone to poor Negro schools all his life. He was comforted to discover that his white class mates were just as ignorant as he was.

John took courses in English because he hoped to become a writer. He also followed his interests in painting and theater. He did well in his studies, was very popular and was active in college political activities.

The most important thing that happened to John in college was the development of a deep belief in the principle of nonviolence. It grew, in part, out of his early religious training and was strengthened by his studies of Christianity and other religions in college.

For John, it wasn't enough to say he was against violence. He felt he had to make a pledge to himself that he would live by his belief. It was a promise to act according to his religious training no matter what the personal difficulties or dangers.

At the same time that his religious feeling was developing, John became aware of the civil rights movement being born in the South. He read about the Reverend

Martin Luther King, Jr., and the bus boycott in Montgomery, Alabama. He was moved by the same things that affected most Americans, white and black—the courage of the black people who were suffering in order to win their rights. John felt very close to those Negroes, not only because of their common color, but because they had common beliefs. When he heard Dr. King speak at a student conference, he was extremely impressed. Here was a man with a moral position that had to do with the real world, with current problems. King gave meaning to John's belief that religion should teach you how to live, not just prepare you to die.

As John's graduation day approached, he realized that he really didn't know what he was going to do next. He had begun to discover that his interests in the arts were really strong and his desire to become a writer was even stronger. But he knew he had a lot to learn, so he decided to major in English and stay at college for another year. He got more and more interested in the college theater group, and half way through his fifth year he decided that when he graduated he would move to New York City, write plays, and someday become famous. Even though he thought of the civil rights struggle as the most important movement in the country, he still didn't know what it had to do with his life.

Chapter 2

FACING THE MOB

The spring of the next year something happened to change John's life greatly. A white girl had entered the university after being expelled from a southern college for engaging in civil rights activities with a group called SNCC, the Student Nonviolent Coordinating Committee.

Because segregation was so wide spread in southern Illinois, Negroes always had trouble finding public places that would serve them food or rent them rooms. Some all white towns even had "Sundown Laws" on their books, which meant that Negroes had to get out of town by sunset.

This girl decided it might be a good idea to start a SNCC chapter at the college, partly as a place for civil rights workers to stop off as they traveled through southern Illinois and also as a base of operations for starting an attack against segregation in the area. Someone suggested she see John.

"I'm from SNCC. Let's do something," she said.

John really wasn't interested. "Look, I've done my bit. We had our own little campaign here and straightened out Carbondale. We got the restaurants to serve Negroes. I don't go in much for sit-ins. I don't mean to put you down, but I think the main thing groups like SNCC accomplish is to make their members feel better. They do things without thinking and that's not my way. It just isn't any good."

The girl listened to everything he said and then nodded. "Okay. Let's do something."

When John saw that he couldn't talk her out of it, he started to scheme. "I can hook this white girl up with some of these other white folks and let them go off and do something together."

But no matter how hard he tried, he couldn't escape. As he saw the group form and as he met more SNCC kids, he found himself becoming deeply involved. Before long he was chairman of the university's SNCC chapter. The organization chose Cairo, Illinois, for a campaign.

A tightly segregated town at the southern tip of Illinois, Cairo had more in common with Mississippi 150 miles to the south than it did with the rest of Abraham Lincoln's home state. SNCC chose it because they knew it would put up the strongest fight against integration.

The group began organizing Cairo's Negroes and staging sit-ins and other non-violent demonstrations at public places all through the city. They received a great deal of support from black people of all ages, but especially from the young people. As expected, the whites were very much against them, and it was clear that it would take a long time to bring about any changes.

As he went into his final term that summer, John began spending more and more time in Cairo and less and less at college. He had earned most of his credits so he dropped all but his necessary courses and devoted almost all his energies to the Cairo movement. One of John's main interests was mob control. He had many ideas on the subject and had great confidence in his abilities as a leader and in training others.

One night late in July his ideas were put to a difficult and violent test. SNCC had been staging many demonstrations at the town's segregated recreation facilities because they were of special interest to the young people in the movement. The girl who usually led the protests was recovering from a knife wound she had received at a swim-in a few days earlier. John was running that evening's demonstration at the roller skating rink. About 50 people, SNCC workers, local Negro kids, and a new batch of students from the university, had lined up for tickets. The manager had closed the rink rather than let in the integrated group. An angry mob of whites had gathered to watch. Several SNCC people John had helped to train walked back and forth along the line, keeping the protest in order and watching the mob for signs of trouble.

A white student standing in line behind John looked at the mob and whispered, "I'm worried."

John turned around and smiled. "There's nothing to worry about, Larry. We can go on for another hour and then go back to the church for something to eat. We will get back to school before midnight. There isn't going to be any violence tonight."

As John turned around to face the front of the line again he saw that the whole line of people ahead of him was down on the ground. A white man was walking down the line swinging a baseball bat back and forth, knocking people over. John looked behind him and started to say, "I was wrong," but Larry had disappeared.

John found himself standing in the middle of the screaming mob, thinking calmly to himself, "How could I have been so wrong? What do I do now?" He saw a white girl worker being beaten with a chain and others being attacked with bats, knives, and clubs.

It was time to find a policeman. Although several had been standing near all evening, now there wasn't one to be seen. Throughout it all John remained completely cool, trying to figure out what had happened and what to do about it.

"Should I try to protect the people who are being

beaten or should I get our group back together?" he wondered.

Then he remembered that John Lewis, a Negro from Alabama who later became the head of SNCC, was in the demonstration.

"He's faced this kind of mob dozens of times," John thought. "He will know what to do."

He looked around, spotted John Lewis, and ran over to him. The civil rights leader was standing calmly with his hands in his pockets and whistling "We Shall Overcome."

"Oh, my God," John thought, "this man doesn't know what to do *either!*"

At that moment one of the leaders staggered over to them with his head bleeding badly. Now it was obvious to John what had to be done. The injured civil rights workers had to be taken to the hospital. The two leaders quickly began taking car loads of people off for medical treatment, hurrying back for more wounded. The police had turned up again but were doing nothing to help. John would point to a man and say, "Arrest that man with the gun!"

One policeman would say, "What gun?"

Another would ask, "What man?"

John and the others returned to the Negro church that was serving as their headquarters. Miraculously, no one was seriously hurt. John thought for a long time that night about what had happened during those hours of violence. He tried to organize his thoughts and impressions to see what lessons he had learned.

"John Lewis didn't know what to do, so experience doesn't always help. Accident and luck play a big part in what happens. There isn't a way out of every situation. We needed to hold the group together. Once we were scattered we were in trouble. I was never hit because I stayed cool. I was scared when I was expecting violence but when it came I was calm.

"When I act in a play my stage fright leaves me when the lights go on because I get involved in the play. Tonight I got involved with trying to help others, so my fear disappeared. I thought I didn't know what to do, but I *was* doing something. I was staying in control of myself. The way I behaved must have affected the crowd. They left me alone because of my appearance of self-control and authority. But some of the others acted in a way that made the mob attack them. Instead of being calm and friendly, they became nasty. Without realizing it, they teased the mob into attacking. I was left alone. It looks like some of my ideas about nonviolence were right. This is the first time I've had a chance to test them and they seem to have worked for me. But I've got to do a much better job of teaching the others."

In a way, it really didn't matter. The summer term was almost over and soon John would be writing plays in New York with the problems of the movement far behind him. At least he planned it that way.

Chapter 3

A THEATER IS BORN

Toward the end of August, shortly before the day of his graduation, John realized he was about to commit a real "sin." Though he had always felt that a person must act the way he believed, John was about to do just the opposite. He had a deep belief in the principle of nonviolence. He felt that the civil rights movement was putting that principle into practice in the most important struggle in the United States. He believed that his abilities in nonviolent protest could be useful to that great struggle. And yet he was planning to go off and live in New York and be an artist. He was about to turn his back on his beliefs.

Not only that, but writing for white audiences of New York's commercial theater would be going against what he believed he should be doing as an artist. He wanted to write about black people in America, about life in the South for black people, about their fight for freedom.

How could he unless he wrote plays coming from his own experience? He would be like everyone else in the North. He would only know what he read in the newspapers. Unless he went south he could never be much of an artist—or even much of a man.

The time had also come for John to face the problem of the Army. He knew that if he was to remain true to his belief, he must go to his draft board and state that he was opposed to war on religious grounds. He must ask to be listed as a conscientious objector. He knew c.o. was hard to get, but it would be especially difficult for him. He had a very deep, personal faith in God and in a moral code that did not permit violence. But they were not beliefs tied up with any particular religious group. It would be hard in a court of law to convince a judge that he wasn't just a "draft dodger."

Guided by his own conscience and not by other people's ideas of right and wrong, John O'Neal made the two most important decisions of his life. He filed for c.o. with his draft board, and he told SNCC that he wanted to work full time in the South.

"I can go south for a few years," he said to himself, "and then when we get the mess down there all cleaned up, I can go back to being an artist." John had no lack of spirit and courage, but he had much to learn about the problems that lay ahead.

John became a SNCC worker and moved back to Cairo, where he continued working with the program he had helped organize there. He also became involved with a new movement that was blooming just across the Mississippi River in south-east Missouri.

When Cairo's action program was over, he moved to Atlanta, Georgia, as one of SNCC's 20 field secretaries. John's college work and his experience in the movement had given him a great interest in developing leaders. He enjoyed teaching and was very good at it. He ran work shops on methods of nonviolence, he wrote and gave out booklets, he talked with white officials, he organized and led protests. He would work with young people and through them try to involve their parents and others in the black community. He would try to form a simple political organization within the community and develop leaders to run it after he and his fellow SNCC workers moved on to other projects.

In Atlanta and throughout south-west Georgia, he also ran works shops for registering people to vote.

Another part of the SNCC campaign in Georgia that especially appealed to John was the establishment of community programs that had nothing to do with politics. He helped develop community centers built around the arts. He organized singing groups and tried to encourage people to write songs about what they were doing in the movement. It was very satisfying for him to hear some of the fine folk songs that grew out of these efforts.

John realized the problem wasn't just how to help Negroes get what they wanted. It was more than that. They couldn't put into words exactly what they wanted. And protest was not enough. Programs to achieve change had to be created. That would require a proper education and would take a long time.

In November 1963, as a step toward this end, John moved to Tougaloo College, a Negro institution outside Jackson, Mississippi, to help set up a new program to teach grown Negro men and women to read and write.

John had been at Tougaloo a month when a chance meeting took place that was to have a deep effect on his life. John's passion for the theater had not died during his year and a half with SNCC. He was always looking for theater people to talk to, and now at the college he had become involved with a student dramatic group. One evening, a member of the group pointed to a young Negro in the audience and said, "There's a guy you ought to meet. He's Gil Moses, the editor of the *Mississippi Free Press*. He came over from Jackson to review the play for his paper. You two have a lot in common. He writes plays too. He's directed and even acted in New York."

John had heard of the talented 20-year-old from Cleveland who had left college and a promising career in the theater to run the Mississippi movement's newspaper.

Later, John introduced himself to Gil and sat down next to him in the sea of empty seats in front of the dark stage. Sitting in the empty theater, they discussed and argued about the two most important things in their lives—the movement and the theater. John told Gil about his decision to give up his dream of going to New York.

"I came south, feeling that the movement could change the character of the whole nation. All we had to do was expose the horrors of the South to the press, and the nation would recognize the moral right and act to correct the evil. I figured it might take anywhere from two to five years. I had no idea that the problem was so deep and the process of change so slow. Now I know I won't see real changes in five or even ten years. It'll take a life time, which," John added with a smile, "might be a rather short one given the circumstances."

Gil nodded. "I went through that same process myself. Now that I know it's going to take a long time, I've had to think about my plans again. If I'm going to be an artist, I've got to find a way to do it in the South."

John was thoughtful. Then he said:

"I guess a lot of us have come to that conclusion. I keep running into poets and singers down here. I've met more poets in the movement than in college. Maybe the deepest poetry today is the poetry of action. Art just can't be kept apart from life any more."

"I agree," said Gil, "but I haven't figured out a way of living in the South, doing what must be done and still satisfying my need to work and grow as an artist."

"Neither have I. I realize that my own desires are not as important as being useful to the movement. But I have to be true to myself. I just can't give up the theater for good."

Gil shook his head. "I can't either. But I won't settle for the theater as it is now. In our society, theater is treated like an ice cream parlor. People go when they have nothing better to to. It has no real connection to a man's life or his daily bread. Theater should serve a real need *of* and *in* a community of people."

"Well," said John, "if theater means anything anywhere, it means something here! Perhaps theater can be a way of helping the black man create a language to use in bringing about a new society."

Both John and Gil realized that what had begun simply as conversation was now turning into a plan of action.

Gil said, "We shouldn't make up the language or poetry from a distance. We shouldn't bring in ideas from outside. A Negro writer can't live in a white society and reach the southern black community. Negroes don't read James Baldwin, whites do. We've got to provide a place in which black people can learn to speak for themselves."

"I think we should do something," John answered. "If we got together we might be able to make a place for ourselves in the theater and in the South. We could find a way to use theater to change the way black people think of themselves and their lives."

"And," Gil added, "the way everyone, black and white, thinks of theater."

In the weeks that followed, John and Gil had many more conversations and many arguments. They both had their own ideas, and they didn't always agree.

However, in early 1964 their ideas came together as a three part plan for what they called the Free Southern Theater. They would try to add to the Tougaloo Theater Program, run a touring company and organize a community theater program which would include drama, music, dance, and other arts. It was a very ambitious plan, but they had set their goals and standards very high. And they had almost everything they needed to pull it off: youth, enthusiasm, brains, and talent. In fact, the only thing they lacked was money. They figured the least they would need just for the summer was $50,000!

John and Gil went to SNCC with their ideas and were given $300 for a fund raising trip to New York City. For the next three weeks they spoke to everyone they could find who was connected with the theater, telling them all about the Free Southern Theater and asking for their support. Everyone was impressed and excited about the idea. Everyone gave them the names of those who might contribute money. Many important people in the theater agreed to let their names be used. Several people organized a fund raising group called Friends of the Free Southern Theater. But when John and Gil returned to Jackson, they were only $450 richer.

They were rather discouraged but not beaten. At that point, Gil decided to quit the *Mississippi Free Press*, and he and John applied to the Ford Foundation and the Rockefeller Foundation for grants. They requested enough for a full year's operation: $430,000. Ford wrote back that the foundation was very interested but that the plan needed more work. Ever since they had begun to fight for the Free Southern Theater, John and Gil had faced one disappointment after another. They still believed in their dream, but as summer approached they began to lose faith in the chance of making it work.

Then, in June, as hope and enthusiasm were dying, two people appeared to give them faith. Madelyn Sherwood, a good actress and early backer of the movement, arrived at Tougaloo with a film crew to make a fund raising movie for the Free Southern Theater. But school was out, the work shop was over. She found John and Gil drawing up plans.

"Are you guys just going to sit around here and wait until you get the money or are you going to go and *do* something? Your ideas are great, but now you have to get to work. You can't just wait for money which may or may not come. It will come if the work is there."

Madelyn Sherwood made her film and returned to New York. But her greatest help was those few words that gave John and Gil a much needed push. A couple of weeks later, the Ford Foundation sent their theater expert, Jules Irving, to see what the two men who had dreamed up the Free Southern Theater were doing. Irving worked with them day and night for three days on every detail of their program and money needs, down to the number of nails they would need in a year. It was a professional lesson in theater management. He took them very seriously, and he forced them to take themselves even more seriously.

"The Free Southern Theater has got to be a theater, not a 'theater project,'" he told them. "It can't be a half way measure. If you succeed, this could be a very important step in the American theater."

Now there was no holding them back.

"John," said Gil, "we've got to do something, do a play, go on the road, try. We have to start somewhere."

"Right. But we have no money, no actors, no plays. All we have is you and me."

"Well, let's get kids from the movement. There are plenty of summer workers in Mississippi this year."

"True," said John, "and we can't wait until we have the right plays. They haven't been written yet. Maybe they'll grow out of our theater. For now, couldn't we take *In White America* and change it a little?

"We wouldn't need sets or many costumes for that, and we could borrow a few props and lights from the Tougaloo theater, and make extra lights out of large tomato cans painted black on the outside . . ."

They were thrilled. After all the months of discussions, plans, and ideas, they were at last getting some action.

"We don't need money," John said, smiling. "We can live off the land."

"We'll perform the play in towns where the movement's active, and we won't starve."

"Sure, and by choosing those towns we'll know that our

audiences are in motion, trying to change their lives and trying to understand themselves. And that's the kind of audience we want."

"How soon can we be ready?" asked Gil.

John smiled. "We may never know if we don't start."

In ten days, John and Gil put together the Free Southern Theater's first touring company—quite a job. They found six actors among the summer workers and a singer from a folk group. They decided to play all the male Negro roles themselves. They worked on *In White America*, a play that told the story of the Negro in this country from slave days to the present. They bought a used car with most of the money they raised in New York, borrowed a station wagon from SNCC, and got the use of a car owned by one of the cast. On the eighth day the singer, Jackie Washington, had a mild heart attack, and they had to find a replacement.

On the tenth day, they set out at last for their first stop, McComb, Mississippi, 75 miles south of Jackson. It was pouring rain as the three cars filled with props, lights, curtains, costumes, and excited actors arrived at the Freedom House. A crowd of a hundred Negroes had waited patiently in the rain, singing freedom songs and wondering what was in store for them that night.

The company set up quickly and, just as the rain ended, the lights came up and the play began.

Chapter 4

TOURING MISSISSIPPI

As John looked out at the black faces from the side of the stage, he had no regrets that they weren't an audience at a New York opening. Here he had a true dream, and it was being realized on this steamy Mississippi night.

The audience listened to the opening scenes about early slave days in America with the attention of interested pupils. Soon, John hoped, they would be drawn into the play. He heard the words that signaled his entrance.

> In 1831, the slave Nat Turner and his followers turned on their masters in Southampton County, Virginia.

John moved to the center of the stage, which was in darkness. The spots came up and John stood alone in a pool of light. Without props, costumes, or sets, he would have to create the dismal Virginia jail cell to which Nat

Turner had been taken after his capture. With words and gestures, he must create the vision of a man in chains waiting to go to trial and finally death. It wasn't enough to play the part. He had to cast a spell.

All eyes followed Nat Turner as he paced his cell, preparing what he would say to the judge. The audience held its breath as he spoke.

> I had a vision—I saw white spirits and black spirits engaged in battle, and the sun grew dark—the thunder rolled in the heavens and blood flowed in the streams. . . .

There were gasps as he described the killing of the slave masters and their children. Then a hush fell as he spoke of his capture.

> The white men pursued us and fired on us several times. Five or six of my men were wounded, but none left the field. . . . Finding myself defeated . . . I gave up all hope for the present. . . . I was taken, two weeks later, in a little hole I had dug out with my sword.

Then, standing straight and tall, facing the quiet audience, Nat Turner raised his arms slowly as if fighting against a terrible burden and, holding his hands out to the heavens, said proudly,

> I am here loaded with chains, and willing to suffer the fate that awaits me.

The lights dimmed and the audience sat in a silence broken only by a whispered "damn" or "wow." John sensed that he had reached them, that for a moment they had felt themselves truly in the presence of Nat Turner. Maybe they would start to question the usual idea that anyone who acts on his beliefs must be crazy. Maybe they would question, as John did, the view of American history that makes some men of violence like Nathan Hale and General Custer heroes and others like Nat Turner villains and mad men. Most of all, John hoped they would see that just as Nat Turner did what he thought was right and accepted the consequences, they must not let their fear stop them from working in the movement.

Throughout the rest of the performance the local police did their best to remind the audience and the actors that they had something to fear. A police car circled the Freedom House all evening, making as much noise as possible. The noise got more and more on people's nerves, but there was nothing anyone could do about it. At a very moving part of the play the police car came to a stop right behind the audience. The driver turned up his radio and the air was filled with the sound of police calls. On stage Denise Nicholas was playing a fifteen-year-old Negro girl describing what happened when she tried to go to the all white Central High School in Little Rock, Arkansas, in 1957.

> They moved closer and closer. Somebody started yelling, "Lynch her! Lynch her!"

She shouted the mob's lines and then went on with tears in her voice.

> I tried to see a friendly face somewhere in the mob— someone who maybe would help. I looked into the face of an old woman and it seemed a kind face, but when I looked at her again, she spat on me.

The police radio continued to blast, but Denise went on.

> They came closer, shouting, "No nigger bitch is going to get in our school. GET OUT OF HERE!"

Denise screamed the last line at the top of her lungs, directly at the police. She didn't step out of character, but kept right on with the scene. But in that instant, she had expressed the feelings of the crowd, and the fear that the police had tried to build up vanished.

When the play ended, minutes later, the audience clapped warmly. By now it was late and most of them began to leave for their homes. A few gathered around the stage where the tired actors were taking down the lights and packing up the props. A woman and her young son came over to John and said, "We sure are grateful to you folks for showing us your wonderful play. I think we all learned a lot from watching it."

John was pleased by the woman's gratitude. But he knew that they hadn't really reached her. She had learned from the play, but she hadn't really become a part of it. She hadn't recognized that it had come out of her life, that it was a part of her. He realized that this was a difficult challenge. The theater was a foreign form in the rural South. It was hard for a Negro to get involved with a play the way he might with a song or a sermon or some more familiar thing. And the play itself wasn't quite right. It had been written by a white author for a white audience.

But still John and Gil felt they had made a very good start. The cast was happy to be on the road, and as they moved from town to town through Mississippi, the audiences continued to respond with enthusiasm, showing their appreciation by inviting the cast into their homes, feeding them well—though they had hardly enough for their own families to eat—and putting them up for the night. Some didn't trust them at first, others immediately made them feel a part of their community.

The group performed almost once a day through the month of July, before audiences of anywhere from 50 to 500. John learned more and more about the theater and its effect with each performance. He found that the attitude of the audience was often influenced by where the play was put on. If the performance was in a church, the audience was quiet. If it was in an open field, there was a gay atmosphere. When seeing the play in a school, they treated it as an experience in learning. While performing in a dance hall, the actors had to stop the show and remind the noisy crowd that this was theater, not a dance.

How strange theater was to most people was made

In Alabama in 1961, sometimes the only way to get Negroes safely home from meetings was in army trucks. WIDE WORLD

Henry Aronson pours over paper work
in a tiny Mississippi law office.
JOHNSON PUBLISHING COMPANY

Untying his plane,
Henry and a fellow lawyer prepare to fly
to another part of the state to help
release civil rights workers from jail.
JOHNSON PUBLISHING COMPANY

At times the best way to walk through town proved to be by back alleys.

Scenes from the Free Southern Theater's
first production, *In White America,*
a play that tells the story of
the Negro in American history.
FREE SOUTHERN THEATER, BOB FLETCHER and
FREE SOUTHERN THEATER

John O'Neal in a thoughtful moment
between performances.
FREE SOUTHERN THEATER

John plays Purlie and Denise Nichols
plays Missy in *Purlie Victorious.*
TOM WAKAYAMA

Wherever the Free Southern Theater played, people braved white southern rage to watch Negro history come to life on stage. MATT HERRON

A scene from the play *Happy Ending*. BOB FLETCHER

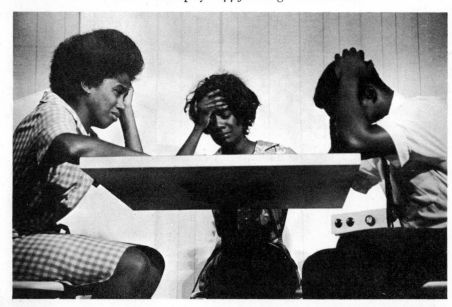

Negro protesters duck away from the powerful spray of fire hoses during the Birmingham demonstrations of May 1963. WIDE WORLD

Eric Weinberger is carried to a police car by state troopers. The incident occurred when Eric and nine others, walking the same route William Moore took when he was shot, crossed the Alabama state line. WIDE WORLD

Lost 45 Pounds In 32-Day Fast Says He "Would Do It Again,"

Visibly weakened by the loss of 45 pounds during a 32-day hunger strike in Alabama's Kilby Prison, Freedom Marcher Eric Weinburger is regaining his strength in Atlanta this week.

The unusually withdrawn, yet boldly dedicated, man slomped over as he sat on the couch at the apartment of a fellow freedom-fighter and related a few details of his foodless stay in jail. He had refused to "co-operate with an unjust system."

Weinburger was one of ten Freedom Marchers arrested as they crossed the Alabama state line enroute to Jackson, Mississippi after the fashion of brutally slain postal employee William Moore.

WEINBURGER

The Marchers were all found guilty of disturbing the peace and fined $200 each plus the costs of court after their 32-day stay in prison. They are all out on appeal bonds.

Weinburger has dedicated himself to working with 71 share-cropping families making leather "tote bags" in the cotton country of Brownville, Tennessee to help supplement their earnings during lean months.

Asked if he would go through the whole thing again, the shallow-faced, bearded figure (he grew it in jail) with a disturbing smile looked up and simply said, "Yeah!"

This article appeared on the front page of *The Atlanta Inquirer* after Eric refused to eat while serving a jail sentence.

A portrait of Eric taken shortly after his fast.

A long line of people kneel and pray during a protest in Selma, Alabama.
WIDE WORLD

In Montgomery, Alabama, demonstrators begin to run for cover as club-carrying troopers ride down on them. WIDE WORLD

Young Negro school children are marched into a jail compound after they were arrested at a voter registration demonstration in Selma. WIDE WORLD

One of the reasons why civil rights workers needed courage in the South was the wide use of dynamite. Here a Birmingham Negro's home has been destroyed by one such blast. WIDE WORLD

clear to John one day when they were performing in a little movie house. Young people were studying the sign outside: "A Real Live Play." John heard one boy ask, "Does that mean they're going to use real bullets?"

The police left the group alone as they traveled from place to place. That summer the movement was so active in Mississippi that the police had problems far more serious than the Free Southern Theater. Still, the tiny group was often followed by police cars and was given many traffic tickets for no good reason.

After a few weeks Jackie Washington recovered enough from his heart attack to join the group. By now the other actors were tired and suffering from colds. They performed every night and then were on the road again. As if their schedule wasn't heavy enough, they would now and then get a request to stage an additional performance.

One day, early in August, they had finished an afternoon performance on the porch of the Freedom House in the little town of Ruleville and were looking forward to an evening of rest. As they were packing up, John received a call from a movement leader in Indianola, a city about 25 miles to the south.

"We've been hearing a great deal about your theater, and the people here are just dying to see it. Could you put on the play here tonight?"

"The cast is pretty tired and some of us aren't feeling too well . . ." John began.

"Folks will come in from all over the county. It's not every day they get to see a play. It would mean a lot."

John sighed. He had no choice.

"All right, we can be there around five o'clock."

"Oh, that's wonderful. I can promise you a very good audience."

When John told the cast, they muttered and complained about the heat and their illnesses. That night, as they set up in a little Freedom School assembly room, they were still coughing, sneezing, and moaning. The room, which held about 90 people, was filled an hour before the play was scheduled to begin. The Negroes milled around, talking and joking with one another. Suddenly, 15 minutes before the performance, a hush fell over the crowd as a group of 40 whites walked in and took seats right in the middle of the front section.

John looked at them in surprise. Behind them he could see that the chief of police had stationed himself at the main entrance to the hall and policemen were guarding all the exits. John looked out the window and saw about 80 more policemen surrounding the building. The whites in the audience were neatly dressed men, ranging in age from 25 to 60. John, Gil, and one of the local people went over to the chief of police and asked what was going on.

"They're here to see the show," he answered simply.

"And what about all the police?" John asked.

"We are here to protect them."

74

John and Gil went back stage and had a conference with the cast. "Do you think they are members of the Klan?" someone asked.

"Could be," said John, "but tonight they don't seem to be klanning or kluxing, or whatever you call it."

"What do you think we should do?"

"We wouldn't want to disappoint them."

"After all, the play was written for a white audience."

"If they came to see the show, they're going to see it!"

The entire cast had forgotten about their illnesses and couldn't wait to get out on the stage. Jackie Washington went out and did his before-the-show songs. He did all the movement songs louder and with more feeling than ever before.

> *Don't Tom to Mr. Charlie*
> *Don't listen to his lies*
> *'Cause black folks haven't got a chance*
> *Unless they organize.*
> *Which side are you on?*

He was aiming his words right at the group of whites, and the Negroes loved it. News had spread around the little community and the place was packed. Three hundred people stood jammed together inside. Every window was filled with black faces looking in.

Then the lights went down and the play began. Every member of the cast felt, "What this is all about is right down there in the front row." It was the best performance they gave all season. Every word seemed to take on new meaning. The cast felt it, and the audience felt it too. When John played Nat Turner and lifted up his chains, he was standing face to face with the man who kept Indianola's black community in the chains of segregation.

Then, in the second act, John got particular pleasure out of playing one of his favorite roles, W. E. B. Du Bois, the Negro leader who spoke out against Uncle Toms early in the century and later helped found the NAACP. John felt his words were as true today as when Du Bois said them 50 years earlier. He let the speech build slowly and then spoke the final words directly to every black man in the room.

> The way for a people to gain their rights is not by throwing them away and insisting that they do not want them; Negroes must insist, in season and out of season, that voting is necessary to modern man, that black boys need education as well as white boys.

The Negroes in the audience cheered loud and long when the speech ended. The tiny room almost shook from the sound. The whites sat without expression, as they had throughout the performance. But their presence, rather than holding back the rest of the crowd, seemed to add to its pleasure.

The whites did give one of the actors some bad moments, however. Eric Weinberger, a white civil rights worker, was especially good as Senator Ben Tillman, of

South Carolina, who in 1907 delivered a speech in defense of lynching from the floor of the U. S. Senate. Eric, who himself had been beaten several times in the South, performed the role with such understanding that Negroes, not used to the magic of theater, thought he *was* a man like the senator. After each performance they would shy away from him until they discovered that he was "all right." But tonight Eric was playing the role for the first time in front of white men who probably shared the senator's opinions. He played it with his usual fire, first describing in great detail the imagined attack on a white woman by a black man, and then calling for lynch mob justice.

> And shall such a creature, because he looks like a man, appeal to the law? Shall men stand up and demand for him the right to have a fair trial and be punished in the regular course of justice? I believe he has put himself outside the pale of the law, human and divine.

Sweat poured down Eric's face as he spoke. "Is it the hot lights or those whites up front," he wondered. "I hope they don't think I'm making fun of the white man and take a shot at me. They've been pretty quiet so far. If any speech can set them off, this is it." Eric continued, his voice filled with the senator's passion and hate.

> It is idle to reason about it. It is idle to preach about it. Hot blood rushes to the heart. Civilization peels off us, any and all of us who are men, and we turn into the original

77

savage type whose feelings under such circumstances have always been to kill! kill! kill!

Whatever the whites felt at the moment they kept well hidden. They remained silent until the end of the play. Then they joined in the clapping, and as they filed out past the actors, they paid a few brief compliments. "Excellent," one said to Eric. "Good show," another told John.

The Negroes naturally had a great deal more enthusiasm. They had felt more a part of the play than any audience had before. "We were doing it together tonight," John thought happily. "We were telling the white man with our words and they were telling him by cheering our words. I'd give anything to know what those white cats thought."

The next morning John found out. A magazine writer had seen the performance and had been curious too. She investigated and told John what she had discovered. "The White Citizens Council had wanted to find out if the play was communist inspired, so they came to see for themselves. They were quite serious about it. They decided that it was indeed communist propaganda, although they had to admit that the quality of the work was higher than they had expected."

John laughed. "Every word in that play was written or spoken by such dangerous men as Thomas Jefferson and Woodrow Wilson."

Later on that week, the company arrived in Greenville, the largest city in the Mississippi Delta. There wasn't much of a movement here. The black community didn't want to rock the boat. So John wasn't sure how the play would be received. For most of the day the cast rested and had a doctor examine their various illnesses and give them shots, cough syrup, and pills. By the time they got to the Baptist Church that was to be their theater, they were feeling pretty good.

In an effort to involve the audience more in the performance, Gil had changed the opening of the play. It began with an empty stage and the actors sitting throughout the audience. The actors called out their first lines from the audience. Then, while Denise sang a freedom song, the cast filed onto the stage. The idea was to help the audience feel that the play came from them and was a part of them because it was their story.

That night the opening was especially good. Once he was at the front of the stage and was facing the audience, John waited for his first signal to start. When it didn't come, he began to wonder what was wrong. He waited nervously and then heard some laughing in the audience. He turned around to see what had happened. There on the stage behind him was a black man he had never seen before, standing, straight as an arrow and stony faced, his arms folded across his chest like Chief Sitting Bull.

"This man was really convinced by the opening," John

thought. "He came up to take part too. What are we going to do?"

The whole cast was surprised. They had got the man involved in the magic of the theater, but they weren't sure what to do about it now. Finally, Jackie Washington got him off the stage and the play went on.

After the performance the man came back to help them strike the set. He explained that he had been a little drunk when he got up on the stage. John could tell by talking to him that he was similar to many Negroes in the South who are bright but for some reason cannot deal with the situation they find themselves in. Instead of giving in or fighting back they "flip out," become the "town drunk" or "village idiot." John had always wanted to write something about people like that.

"You know," he told John, "when I walked up there I knew exactly what I wanted to say. But the lights hit me and I just forgot."

His words affected John very deeply. He thought about it for a long time afterward.

"He's the one our theater is all about. What we are doing is for him and all the others who can't find the words for what they want to say. If we are successful, maybe some day they won't 'forget.'"

Chapter 5

A NEW VOICE FOR THE SILENT

When the Free Southern Theater finished its first tour toward the end of August, it had brought *In White America* to 23 towns in 26 days. Everywhere, people responded, and everyone expressed the hope that the group would come back soon with another play. Both John and Gil were pleased with the crowds and with the quality of the performances. However, they had set very high goals for their theater. They spent long hours talking about the tour and trying to judge its effect.

"Some of the communities had discussions about the play, but we were usually gone by then," said Gil. "We don't really know how well we got through to them."

John added, "Next time we should make the discussion a part of every evening's performance. That way we can see what's working and what isn't."

"We're getting some people interested in the idea of theater as a means of expression. There are all those little theater groups that sprang up in the Delta after we passed through. They wrote their own plays, on the model of *In White America*, and considering we were the first theater they ever saw, they did quite well. The Freedom School kids in McComb toured New York and Washington with a play they wrote to raise money for the McComb project."

"I know," said John, "and the one I saw that those kids from Holly Springs put on in Meridian was really good. They did a scene of Medgar Evers' family the night he was killed. They had a real depth of understanding. They made it clear they felt nothing was going to be done about the murder. I think they really used theater to express a sense of the movement."

"We've got to encourage that sort of thing a lot more, spend more time in each town, a week if possible. Run some work shops, do a few plays, really try to get our ideas across."

"If only we had more money and more people," Gil added. "What we should have is someone who could stay in the community after we move on to work with the people, help them organize their own theater groups."

John laughed bitterly. "If we don't raise some money pretty soon, we'll be out of business altogether."

In the course of the tour, about $5000 had come in from their fund raising sources in New York. But they had spent it all and their bank account was empty. So John and Gil spent the next four weeks in New York trying to raise money and find actors. When they returned they had hired five more actors. With the help of the Friends of the Free Southern Theater, which included Paul Newman, Harry Belafonte, Robert Ryan, Theodore Bikel, Ossie Davis, Ruby Dee, Diahann Carroll, Brock Peters, Diana Sands, and Madelyn Sherwood, they had raised $6000. But the second tour was a much longer one and they needed $40,000 to complete it. They planned to spend several days in each town doing two plays and running a theater work shop.

Even though they didn't have enough money on hand to get through the tour, John and Gil decided to go ahead anyway. After much discussion they chose the two plays. One was *Purlie Victorious*, a play by Negro actor Ossie Davis, which had a direct connection with the movement. It was about a Negro preacher named Purlie who returns to his southern home to claim money due him from a white farm owner in order to buy a church and preach freedom from the cotton fields.

The second play was Samuel Beckett's *Waiting for Godot*, a play with almost no plot. *Purlie Victorious* was an obvious choice because it came out of the Negro experience and black audiences would identify with it easily. But *Godot* was a difficult play for any audience to understand. And as far as its content went, it didn't connect directly with the movement at all. Yet, John and

Gil agreed that it was a brilliant play and a great work of art. They felt that they should try it.

"If they can take *Godot*," John had said, "they can take anything."

Although John had been deeply involved in the Free Southern Theater for almost a year now, it was not his only love. The year before, at a civil rights demonstration in Jackson, he had met a Mississippi girl named Mary Felice Lovelace. She was a gifted painter and was studying at Howard University, a Negro college in Washington, D.C., which had become the source of many civil rights workers and movement activities. John had stayed in touch with Mary in the months that followed, seeing her whenever he could, writing to her, meeting her at civil rights conferences, spending Christmas vacation with her. Now that she was through with college and back in Jackson, John had a chance to spend more time with her.

Everything seemed to be going well for John. He had his theater, his place in the movement, and he was in love. Then one day late in September a letter arrived that changed everything. That afternoon he took Mary for a long walk in the park and told her about it.

"I just got a notice from my draft board. It's denied my final appeal. I'm supposed to report for service in the Army day after tomorrow."

"Oh, John, I'm sorry. What are you going to do?"

"Well, I will appear, but I'm going to refuse to serve.

My feelings about serving in the military haven't changed any."

They walked on the tree lined paths in silence, paying no attention to the angry stares of people who didn't like the presence of a black couple in "the white folks' park."

Then John laughed sadly. "This may be your last chance to marry me, you know."

"What do you mean?"

"They can put me in jail for five years for this. You wouldn't want to wait that long, would you? Let's get married right away."

"Be serious, John."

"I am serious, honey. I know it doesn't sound very romantic. And I know it sounds like I just want to marry you because they aren't taking married men. But you've got to believe me. I love you and I'm serious about wanting to marry you."

Mary thought for a long time; then she shook her head. "I'm sorry, John. I can't do it like that."

John was very disappointed. "All right," he said, "but I'm not giving up."

Two days later John reported to the Army Induction Center in St. Louis. When the commanding officer read the oath, John refused to take the one step forward that would mean that he had joined the Army.

"You can't do that!" the officer shouted. He called the draft board.

"This has never happened before," the board said.

Next he called the FBI and, when an agent arrived, demanded, "Arrest that man!"

The FBI agent explained John's rights to the angry officer. "I'm afraid you'll have to release him. We can't arrest him without a warrant. Before we can get a warrant, his local board has to rule on it and refer it to a grand jury. If the jury accuses him, then we can get a warrant and arrest him."

"How long will that take?" the officer asked.

The FBI man frowned. "It could take months."

John returned to New Orleans the next day. The problem was put off but far from solved. He had acted out of deep feeling and now he knew he would have to face the consequences. He thought of Nat Turner.

"He took his stand for violence and I took mine against it, and we both end up jailed by an angry society. I only hope I can be as brave about the fate that awaits me."

But he couldn't spend his time worrying about his case. He had an excellent American Civil Liberties Union lawyer doing that for him. He had to spend his energies on the two things that mattered to him most—the theater and Mary.

The Free Southern Theater had moved to New Orleans, and was practicing for *Purlie* and *Godot*. Happily, Mary was working for CORE, the Congress of Racial Equality, in New Orleans, and John saw a great deal of her. At the end of four weeks the cast was ready to go on the road and Mary had changed her mind and agreed to become John's wife.

The last week in October 1964 the Free Southern Theater set off on its second tour with its three cars, a company of nine, high spirits, and a small bank account.

Their first stop was again McComb, Mississippi. The first day they performed *Purlie Victorious* and, as they had expected, the audience loved it. The Negroes easily identified with the characters and in the discussion that followed made comments out of their own experience such as, "That fellow Purlie. Just like a preacher, always hiding behind a woman's skirts."

The next night the group put on *Waiting for Godot*, knowing that it might not reach the audience at all. In it two men in tramp clothes wait on a country road for someone called Godot. They complain, argue, fall asleep, have bad dreams, and wonder why they are waiting for Godot. A man and his slave enter briefly and then leave after Lucky, the slave, played by John, recites a long speech. The two men wait throughout the second act, while trading funny hats and pretending to be slave and master. Lucky and his master return, and when they fall to the ground, the others try to help them up, only to fall down themselves. Shortly after, Lucky and his master leave again. Godot sends word that he won't be coming today, but will come tomorrow. As the play ends, the two men are still waiting.

When the play ended and John asked if anyone would

like to say anything about it, there was silence. Then a Negro in the audience stood up slowly and began to speak. He looked about 35 or 40, but he could have been much younger. He spoke with great difficulty, trying to find words to express his feelings. Most of what he said was lost, but some words came through clearly. "No more . . . white man . . . master. Man . . . slave . . . no more."

It was a moving experience and it was to be repeated often as the theater moved through Mississippi. People were beginning to search for ways to say how they felt, to speak for themselves. The discussions were not directed, there were no right ways or wrong ways of understanding the plays. The important thing was to get the audience to think and to express thoughts.

The best expression came one night between the acts. Mrs. Fanny Lou Hamer, one of the local leaders of the movement, stood up and addressed the crowd.

"I sure am glad that John O'Neal and Mr. Moses brought this play here. Because every day you see people standing around at the barber shop and at the pool hall and in the bars dressed just about like these people, waitin' for something. They must be waitin' on Godot. But you can't wait for other people to bring you your freedom. You gotta get out there and take it, 'cause we've been waitin' 300 years and we haven't got it yet!"

Chapter 6

PAINFUL VICTORY

When John returned from the theater's highly successful second tour, he immediately went to the CORE office to see Mary. When he got there, he was told that she was in jail but would be getting out later in the day. Once the necessary arrangements for her release had been made, John went to pick her up.

"What happened?" he asked calmly. Going to jail was much too common in the civil rights movement to get excited about it.

"I went into a diner with a white guy from CORE to buy a drink. They refused to serve us, and when we wouldn't leave, they called the cops."

John smiled. "Look, if we are both going to be around for that wedding, we better stay out of jail for a while."

On February 4, 1965, three weeks before they were

scheduled to be married, John got a call from his parents.

"The FBI have been here looking for you. They have a warrant for your arrest!"

John was in New York City at the time. The following day he and the other members of the company were doing a performance of *Waiting for Godot* to raise badly needed money for the Free Southern Theater. What if he were arrested now? But he was not going to run away from justice. He called his lawyer, who got in touch with the FBI in Illinois and told them that John was prepared to surrender. He was told that agents had already been sent to New York after him. At 7:00 the night of the performance John arrived at the New School Theatre, where the play was being given. A group of people were milling around, talking to each other. Off to one side John saw two men wearing trench coats and hats, standing silently with their hands in their pockets.

"That's got to be the FBI," John said to himself.

Jamie Cromwell, who directed and acted in *Godot*, rushed over to him and whispered, "The FBI is here to arrest you. We told them we don't know where you are. Go back stage and get in costume. We will just start the show and they'll have to wait."

John laughed. "No, Jamie. These guys will come right up and stop the show. I've got to go tell them."

Jamie shook his head. "Well, I hope you know what you are doing."

"So do I," said John as he walked over to the two

agents. He knew he had a lot of fast talking to do. He moved up to them and began his pitch.

"Hey, I'm John O'Neal. You are looking for me. My lawyer's been trying to reach you all day to tell you I'm ready to surrender. Look, we've got this show to do. So you can stay until after it's over, because there's nobody to take my place. This is our only chance to make money for this thing. You see, we do plays free all over the South, and it means a great deal to a lot of people. If we blow this show tonight, we've blown our only fund raising device."

John was afraid if he paused the surprised agents would recover and arrest him so he kept right on.

"You've got to wait. You can even have free tickets!"

John stopped and the two FBI men huddled together for a minute. "Okay," one of them said finally, "we'll wait."

After the performance, the cast remained on stage for a discussion with the audience. The agents moved up to the front of the stage to prevent John from escaping. They kept pointing to their watches and looking at John. John kept whispering, "Okay, okay." Finally he went down to his dressing room. The FBI men came with him and watched him take off his white clown make-up with cold cream. The agents were rushing him, so when they finally hurried him into the car his face was marked with white and there was still gray coloring in his hair.

As they drove to the Federal Detention Center, John

asked them what they thought of the show. One agent, a tall, quiet man from Oklahoma, said, "Do you think it was all right to use all that language in front of the women?"

John was surprised. He tried to think of what "language" had offended the man. The play had a few "damns" in it, but it wasn't a dirty play.

"These guys probably have as little experience with theater as our audiences in Mississippi," John thought. Then he laughed to himself. "Maybe on our next tour we should schedule some shows just for FBI agents!"

John spent the night in jail, which probably bothered him less than it did his cell mate, who didn't know what to make of the black man with strange white marks down his face and gray powder in his hair!

The next day he was released on $500 bail.

"It's funny," he thought as he left the Detention Center. "In four years of civil rights work in the South, I've never spent a day in jail. Now I come to New York and they lock me up."

But the performance had raised $3500 for the Free Southern Theater, so John felt it was a small price to pay.

John and Mary got married at the end of the month. Although it was a day of great happiness, there was the threat of a trial ahead for John. Mary hadn't really grasped how serious John's position was until she went with him to the office of one of his lawyers. The attorney painted a very dark picture that day.

"You are probably going to lose this case, John. You can't just tell the Army to go to hell and expect to get away with it. Now, you don't want to spend five years in jail and pay a $10,000 fine . . ."

Mary was shocked. John had told her before but it hadn't sunk in. The lawyer continued.

"The wisest thing for you to do is to think it over and not go through with it. It really looks bad for you now. So give it up. Tell them you'll go in the Army. They'll give you a job where you won't have to fight."

John could see that Mary was scared. He wasn't feeling too well himself. But it wasn't the first time he had been frightened. He had learned to accept fear as a fact of life and to go on doing what he believed in in spite of it. Now he shook his head slowly.

"No. I couldn't do that. When I decided not to go into the Army, it wasn't because it was the easiest, safest, or most practical thing to do. It was because my deepest religious feelings make it impossible for me to be part of the military. I hope I don't have to go to jail. But if living by my beliefs requires it, I'll just have to go."

The lawyer smiled. "We are doing our best to see that you don't have to go. It looks bad, but not hopeless."

In the months that followed, John kept busy with the Free Southern Theater. The company had grown and so had the problems. For the third tour they had increased the company to 25 and the number of plays to three. A larger work shop program was planned with more time to be spent in each community. Their cost was now $180,000 and they had only $10,000 in the bank. The problems were enormous. Someone had to deal with them full time, so while the company was on the road, John stayed behind in New Orleans with all the headaches. He often felt left out, and he was itching to get back on the stage again. But someone had to run the theater, and no one else was willing or able to do it.

John's most constant worry was money. There never seemed to be enough to meet the weekly salaries of $850 for the 25 people. Often the books showed a balance of zero, and John would be afraid that they couldn't go on. Then, suddenly, some money would appear. Once a civil rights worker, who had come from California to gather folk material, walked in and handed John a check for $5000. Two weeks later, when the situation again looked bad, John opened a letter and found a check for $10,000!

When he wasn't sweating it out in New Orleans, John joined the company on the road to see how things were going. He found that some very interesting changes were taking place. For one thing, the character of the audience was different. In earlier tours, most of the people who came to the shows were the poorest back country Negroes —people who had joined the movement to help raise themselves up from poverty at the bottom of southern society. Now, more and more members of the small Negro urban middle class—the teachers and store owners and professional people—were coming. And John noticed more and more people who had seen the theater once, even twice before. The Free Southern Theater had succeeded in developing its own audience and following, separate from the movement, and in bringing together people who never before had been able to get together.

John also got a chance to see how well the theater's community programs were working. While the company was in a town, anywhere from a few days to a week, they would run theater work shops. They would get together with whoever was interested and work with them on simple dramatic projects. The important thing was to get people involved immediately so they didn't worry about turning out polished performances or productions.

The people, from 12 years of age to 35, set up situations and then acted out what they felt would happen. Their ideas came from their own experiences and so usually had to do with the movement. Someone would say, "Let's do a demonstration at a lunch counter." Another would agree. "Okay. I can be the sheriff and you be a civil rights worker." "And I'll be that Uncle Tom policeman who always helps the sheriff." Then they would act out their roles in a scene.

The purpose was not to learn what to do when arrested or how to defend yourself against blows. The work shop scenes were an attempt to get beneath the surface into the feelings of the people involved. Why does the white man attack? How does it feel to be attacked? What makes the sheriff tick?

John was impressed at how the people made up their parts. The sheriff, whom they had all run into in the course of the movement activities, was very well drawn. They often played him as a person to feel sorry for rather than just an evil man. And they could find and act out amusing ideas about the sheriff or the Uncle Toms in the black community.

In a few towns the kids made their scenes into whole shows and performed them in public. People in the black community were finding new ways to express their ideas and feelings. The Free Southern Theater was working.

Still, there was much to be done. They had to find ways to raise more money. They had to cut down on the size of the company. People who could stay in the communities after the group left had to be signed up. They had to find or develop writers within the communities. But John was now more convinced than ever that the project was worth working and fighting for—no matter how hard it would be or how long it would take.

While John worked on the theater's problems throughout the summer and into the fall, his lawyers were fighting legal battles in the courts to keep him out of jail. Finally, on October 24, 1965, his case came to trial.

The first person to speak in the St. Louis court room was the district attorney. He rose quickly and addressed the judge. "Your Honor, we feel justice will best be served in this case if the case is dismissed. We are willing to drop the charges if this man is willing to accept other service."

The judge called John up to the bench and asked him, "Boy? You willing to work in a hospital?"

"Yes, your honor," John answered. "I am willing."

John had won! The government had recognized his legal right to a personal religious belief. He didn't want to leave the theater, but at least he would be doing something for a hospital, religious group, or poverty program. It might also be a good thing that he and his new wife would be getting away from the South for a few years before returning for good.

When John had entered the court house that morning it had been with a feeling of doubt. Now he was leaving it with confidence. The Free Southern Theater might slow down while he was away, but it wouldn't die. Its roots were buried too deeply in the soil of the black communities of the South. He would try to do his service in New York City, near sources of funds and talent, in a job that would allow him to travel and keep in touch with the theater. He would still be able to play a role in its growth, in shaping its aims and achieving its goals. There would be many problems, but he knew that wherever he would go from now on, he would be a part of the Free Southern Theater and it would be a part of him.

THE
ERIC WEINBERGER
STORY

Chapter 1

THE SEARCH

Eric Weinberger marched into Montgomery, Alabama, a city known both as the birth place of the Negroes' struggle for equal rights and as the center of white opposition to it. He moved along in a sea of people—different in race, religion, background, and wealth, yet today united in a single cause. This was the Selma Freedom March in the first week of spring 1965.

The march went through the streets of Montgomery's black community, filling the neighborhood with the sound of joyful freedom songs. Negroes poured off the steps of their shabby houses and joined in the long line of marchers. By the time the Freedom March reached the state capitol building, the crowd had grown to 25,000.

It was a terribly moving moment for Eric. His body carried scars from more than a dozen violent arrests.

Fear and pain had left their mark on him, but there were also many wonderful memories, and this day had brought them back to him. He had seen these faces before—the bright-eyed young people—willing and even eager to lay their lives on the line to get their rights; the grand fathers, too old to benefit from the struggle, yet willing to risk their few remaining years to win a good future for their black grand children; the men and women, kept in ignorance and poverty by a white society, fighting back with dignity and courage.

Eric had heard and sung these songs before—in churches and jails, on marches and demonstrations, at times of triumph and at moments of despair. Now as he stood in the huge crowd, he felt the joy and shared the pride, but it was mixed with sadness. This great civil rights demonstration would be his last. He wasn't needed any more.

Eric was born in New York City in 1932, with all the advantages (or so they seemed at the time) of a white, Jewish, middle-class life. His father was a lawyer and active in the National Association for the Advancement of Colored People and other "good, liberal" causes. His mother was a retired high school teacher. Eric had gone to a public school and after tenth grade, when he was 15, was shipped off to a special program at the University of Chicago where he was to get his degree by age 19.

It was taken for granted he would go on to graduate school and then become a lawyer. It was assumed by his parents, friends, and, for most of his life, by Eric himself that he had an ordinary middle-class future ahead of him. It came as a shock when, after two years at the university, Eric told his parents he was leaving school.

"I could give you a whole lot of reasons, ' he explained, "but the main thing is I just can't stand it."

"But why?" his father asked.

"The place is not human. Their idea of education is stuffing as much knowledge as possible into as many heads as possible as fast as possible. There's got to be more to being a person and more to life."

"So what are you going to do?"

"I want to travel, get a job, see if I can learn about myself and the world on my own."

His mother shook her head. "You'll dig ditches for the rest of your life."

In the years that followed Eric didn't dig any ditches but he did just about everything else. He hitch hiked around the country, sold popcorn in a circus, worked as a bus boy in Philadelphia, was an actor in an off-Broadway theater, and wrote poetry, some of which was published. His parents talked him into going back to school, but when he was 20, he quit for good.

He lived in Greenwich Village for a while and then went out to San Francisco. The "hippie scene" was just beginning there, but Eric didn't find any point to it. He knew he wanted to do something with his life—he just didn't know what.

One day, late in the spring of 1960, working in a Norwalk, Connecticut, printing plant, Eric went out to get a sandwich for his boss. A peace walk was on its way through town. He stopped and watched the 12 marchers with their signs against war and was handed a paper as they passed by. Eric read it with great interest. It explained that the marchers were from a group called the NE/CNVA—the New England Committee for Nonviolent Action which, in addition to peace walks, carried out a program of very direct non-violent action such as boarding submarines as a protest against the arms race.

It sounded a little crazy, but the people on the walk didn't *look* crazy and they were protesting something Eric felt was very dangerous. He began reading all the material the NE/CNVA was putting out and became more and more interested in their work. The committee had a farm in Norwich about ten miles from the submarine base in Groton. Here the group lived and held non-violent training meetings. Eric had a summer vacation coming up, so he decided to spend a few weeks there to see what it was all about.

When he got to the farm, Eric found he was in the company of 16 remarkable human beings, and he was immediately drawn to them. They were intelligent people and, what impressed him most of all, they were doing what they felt was right. They were all serious peace workers whose actions grew out of deep religious faith and a political belief in social change. All through his life, he had known people who had noble beliefs, but these were the first who lived by them completely.

Eric learned a great deal about the group's feelings and also about himself. He had never liked fights as a kid and had discovered that people looked down on him for it. So, even though he knew violence was wrong, he had felt ashamed. Now he realized that refusing to fight could be a strong act rather than a weak one. To say war is wrong, killing is wrong, and I will not, in fact cannot, support the system that makes war is not running away. It is taking a moral stand. A child knows it has to eat long before it knows the reasons why. And Eric had known he could never kill before he knew why.

Eric quit his job at the printing plant and moved to the peace community. For the next six months he worked as a staff member for no pay. His life now had purpose and direction, but he still needed a meaningful way of putting both into action. At the year's end, unhappy events 1000 miles to the south gave Eric his chance. Bob Swann, the group's leader, told him about it.

"Large numbers of Negroes in several farm counties in Tennessee have been registering to vote for the first time since Reconstruction days. The whites have kicked the Negro farmers who registered off the land. Hundreds of families were left without a place to live or a way to earn a living. It's a pretty desperate problem."

"I thought Tennessee was quite a liberal state."

"Some of it is. But in the true black belt areas in the

west, Haywood and Fayette counties, Negroes are treated as badly as in Mississippi 50 miles to the south. Haywood is 60 per cent black, and the whites are afraid of what would happen if the Negroes started voting en masse."

"What's happened to the people who were thrown off the farms?"

"Some are living in shacks and others in large army tents that were given to them. They really need help."

Eric nodded. "I think if we're going to oppose war, we should also fight against the violence being suffered by Negroes. But what can we do? We have no money."

"They need more than money, Eric. They need some way of helping themselves. Up to now all they've had is what the whites allow them to have. They should have an independent way of supporting themselves—a job that will not only make money but build some pride."

"You sound like you have something in mind."

"I do. I heard about a Quaker school teacher up in New Hampshire who designed a leather tote bag, sort of a large shoulder bag, for his students to make and sell. In a short time they sold enough to pay for a trip to Mexico for the whole class. I have an idea that kind of project might work in Tennessee. How would you like to go down and give it a try?"

"But I have no experience in leather work," said Eric.

"That's the whole point of these bags. They're designed so any one can make them. All you have to do is get some

103

Negroes organized, show them how to do a couple, and arrange to have them sold. It could work."

"There's only one way to find out," said Eric. "When do I leave?"

"That's up to you. From now on, you're on your own."

Eric was excited. This was the opportunity he had been waiting for. But he also had plenty of doubts. He knew so little about the South and nothing about running a project like this. What little he had read about the small civil rights movement that existed at that time had given him the impression that it was being carried out by a handful of very brave young people. Would he have that kind of courage? Would he be able to act according to his beliefs? Eric knew those frightening questions could only be answered in the South.

He went up to see the Quaker teacher in New Hampshire to learn how to make the bags. Then he went to New York City and discussed his project with the leaders of CORE. CORE's main activities in the South were sit-ins and other non-violent protests aimed at ending segregation. But Eric's plan interested them. They agreed to print up notices about the tote bags and they gave Eric $100 for his trip to Tennessee.

Finally, in December 1960, Eric set out for the South on a mission that was to have great importance not only in the lives of hundreds of black people but also in his own.

Chapter 2

WELCOME TO BROWNSVILLE

Eric followed the tall Negro across the muddy field, avoiding the deep puddles left from a recent rain. Ahead, five large army tents with stained, sagging canvas stood dark against the winter sky.

In the North they were thought of as monuments to the courage of Negroes who stood up to the whites and registered to vote. But now, as one of the leaders of the movement showed him around Haywood County's Tent City, Eric saw that the cold ugly structures, which let in no sunlight when it was fair and a great deal of water when it rained, were all that 50 human beings could call home.

Built on wooden platforms in the open field of a Negro owned farm, the tents were divided into two sections that served as kitchen and living room during the day and cramped bedrooms at night. Each of the leaders of Haywood County's small movement lived in a tent with his family—about ten people, infants and old people, living under one roof.

"Hundreds of us who registered were thrown off the farms after we got the cotton and corn harvested this fall," Eric's guide explained. "Some left the county, some found shacks to live in, and the rest of us stay here." He could see that Eric was looking a little unhappy, so he added, "These tents really aren't much worse than the shacks we used to live in. We have to fetch water in cans from a half a mile down the road, but we manage."

"What about food?" Eric asked. "How do you get along without any income?"

"We get surplus food from the government. It doesn't taste very good, but it's not so bad. Some families live off one of the old folks' Social Security. That's $50 a month. It isn't much for ten people, but it helps. A few work for a Negro land owner once in a while, and from time to time the whites hire some."

"But I thought the whites wouldn't hire any of you."

"That's not quite true. Some white folks just can't pass up a bargain. They hire our people at a lower rate. Two dollars a day instead of the usual three."

Eric couldn't believe it. Two dollars for a 12 hour day of hard labor in the fields. He had been afraid that the amount of money his project might earn them would be only a drop in the bucket. Now he realized the bucket had been almost empty for a very long time.

"But look on the bright side of it," Eric's companion said. "Over 800 black folks voted last November. And that's 800 more than ever voted here before."

Eric's base of operations was Brownsville, Tennessee, a town of 5000. Brownsville had such a bad reputation that middle-class Negroes driving from Memphis to Nashville would leave the main highway to avoid passing through the city.

During his first few days in Brownsville, Eric met with many of the Negroes, telling them about his project and signing up women to make the bags. Many of them were suspicious of Eric. They couldn't see why a white man wanted to help them. But they needed the money badly, so they agreed to go along with him.

Eric started looking for a central location to store materials and carry out the first steps of production. The owner of a store in Brownsville's Negro section gave him the use of the upper floor of his building, an old loft that was used as a Masonic Hall twice a month and left empty the rest of the time. The large, dusty room became the headquarters of the Haywood Handicrafters League and, with the addition of a small cot, Eric's new home.

To get the project going, Eric taught several of the women living in the tents how to make the bags. He had brought $20 worth of dark brown leather with him. He laid it out on the room's long meeting tables and carefully measured out the pattern of the bags.

After cutting the pieces of leather, he showed the ladies how to use the simple tools and materials he had brought: an awl, like an ice pick, for hammering small holes in the leather; a pair of heavy needles for sewing the bags together; a leather punch for making larger holes; small spools of wax thread, and brass rings.

He started stitching one bag to show them how it was done. He wasn't very good at sewing, but the bags were designed so that all the stitching was on the inside. No matter how badly it was done, the result was a handsome, useful tote bag and, most important of all, a tote bag that would sell.

"It's so simple," Eric thought to himself with a smile, "even an educated, middle-class white boy like myself can make one."

Eric had the ladies take turns using the tools and materials, stitching and assembling the bags. Later they would work on the bags at home. But for now, Eric just wanted to teach them and see if the whole idea was practical. By the end of the day, he had his answer. The women had put together four well made tote bags.

Eric's work was just beginning. He had to take the bags back up north and try to find a place to sell them. And he had to find a place that would sell him leather on credit. Already, they had used up their $20 worth of leather; and the Haywood Handicrafters League had no capital, not a cent for buying more materials.

On his third day in Brownsville, shortly before he had planned to return north, Eric made his first mistake. He did not know that civil rights workers should stay out of the white section of southern towns. He was driving the big old carry-all station wagon, which he had borrowed from NE/CNVA, when he found himself in the center of Brownsville, a half a block from the town square. He noticed that a police car had begun to follow him, so he slowed down. When he reached the square the policeman forced him to stop at the side of the road. After looking Eric over and checking his driver's license, the policeman pointed to the gray stone building in the center of the square and said, "You'll have to come over to the court house with me."

Eric followed the officer through the entrance and into a large room where a sheriff sat behind an old wooden desk reading a newspaper. The policeman whispered something to the sheriff, who rose and came over to Eric, who was worried but not alarmed.

"What are you doing here?" the sheriff asked.

Eric assumed they already knew why he was in town, and since he had nothing to hide anyway, he decided to tell the truth.

"I'm here helping Negroes who were put off their farms set up a self-help project. I'm teaching them to make leather shoulder bags," he explained calmly.

"That shouldn't upset them," he thought. "After all, the whites are always saying that the Negro should learn to stand on his own two feet."

"Come with me," the sheriff said, leading Eric down a dimly lit hall and into a small room. As Eric entered, a heavy steel barred door clanged shut behind him.

"I'm going to have to hold you for a while."

Before Eric could say anything, the sheriff had disappeared. Civil rights workers who had been in the movement for some time always told people where they were going and called in once they got there safely. If their call's didn't come in, their friends would get a lawyer and go looking for them. But no one knew where Eric was. No one knew he was in danger.

A few minutes later, a guard turned a key in the lock and swung the door open. "Come on," he said.

For the first time, Eric's belief in nonviolence was put to the test. He felt it was just as wrong to go along with evil as it was to be evil. Faced with a real situation where this belief had meaning, he didn't hesitate.

"No," he said to the guard simply.

The man roared. "I said get out of there!"

Eric shook his head. "If you want to put me in jail, that's your business. But I'm not going to help you do it."

"Oh, a wise guy." The guard, a fat man but with a powerful build, walked into the cell and grabbed Eric by the arm. As he tried to pull Eric through the door, the slender prisoner went limp. The guard released his grip and Eric fell to the floor. He kicked Eric hard in the ribs but Eric refused to move. The guard went away for a moment and returned with the sheriff.

The hours that followed were a time of agony and terror for the young civil rights worker. In an effort to get him to do as they said, the police turned Eric's cell into a torture chamber. They stuck him with an electric rod made for moving cattle. The cattle prod seared his flesh and sent an electric shock into his body, making his muscles jump. They threatened to cut his throat with a knife. They fastened a metal band around his wrist and tightened it until his hand was blue. Then they dragged him around on the floor until the blood supply to his hand was cut off.

Although the pain was often almost more than he could bear, Eric tried to remain calm, answer their questions, and explain the reasons for the way he behaved.

"I'm not going to do as you want . . . it's nothing against you . . . I know you're doing what you think is right. But I'm doing what I think is right . . . I don't feel I was breaking the law . . . I came down here to start a self-help program so these Negroes can earn a living. I think it's a proper thing to do. It's the only thing I intend to do."

After a while the police gave up trying to get Eric to do as they wanted. They dragged him to his cell and threw him in for the night.

The following day they went to work on him again,

this time trying to carry out certain police rules. He wouldn't stand up in front of their camera, so they photographed him lying on the ground. Finger printing Eric was even more difficult. They ended up tying him to a chair with heavy ropes, then sitting on him. They had less success with their questions.

"Where are you staying?"

"With some black people."

"Who are they?"

"They might get in trouble if I tell you, so I won't."

Once in a while they tried to reason with him.

"It's not our custom for white people to stay with black people. So you can understand why we get so upset about it, can't you?"

"I can understand why you are upset, but I can't understand the custom. Why is it such a terrible thing?"

At that point they would scream at him. "But they stink! Anyone who could stay in a place like that must have something wrong with him."

Eric knew they wouldn't listen to facts, but he tried anyway.

"No. I don't think they stink. The family I'm staying with bathes as often as anyone else. They're poorer than most, but they're doing okay. They seem like pretty good people to me."

The policemen just couldn't believe their ears. They would either look at him in dumb surprise or get violent.

After a few hours they dumped him back into his cell and left him alone.

Eric spent the next day in his cell, waiting for them to come and get him. The guards played on Eric's fear by talking to each other just loudly enough for him to hear them. "Ain't never been a year gone by that I didn't kill at least one nigger."

"I figure I've shot about eight myself."

"Why don't we throw that nigger lover off the Talla-hatchie Bridge?"

"Good idea. The kid will meet a lot of his nigger friends off there. I've lost count of how many we've dumped there."

"Before your time, back in '40, we lynched a nigger over by Hatchie Bottom for trying to vote. Left him face down in the swamp."

Eric knew they weren't joking. He had heard that most of the lynching in the South had been done by the police. Now he was sure of it. Violence had never been a part of his life. It surprised and frightened him that these people could laugh and boast about it.

He couldn't see how the Negroes in the South, whether they were civil rights workers or not, could live with this kind of terror day in day out. The main duty of a southern policeman was to "keep the niggers in their place," and they did it with violence or by threat-ening violence. Eric decided that human beings *can* live with a great amount of terror. The fear doesn't go away

—life just goes on in spite of it. Even Eric, experiencing it for the first time, found that it hadn't forced him to give up. He knew why he had come to the South and that he had to keep on working in Brownsville.

"That is, if I ever get out of here alive," he thought.

Brownsville's sheriff, who had stayed out of sight while his helpers tried to get across the "message" to Eric, had been acting according to an old southern tradition—the idea that the South could do anything it wanted to the people it had down there, and no one in the North or the federal government would do anything about it. But now the rules were changing.

CORE had found out about Eric's being in jail and had sent down a lawyer to get him out. By law the police could hold someone for 72 hours without charges. CORE and their lawyer raised such a fuss that the sheriff had to admit he had no charges to press. Eric was released at the end of his third day in jail.

As the policeman led Eric out of the court house, he finally put the "message" into words.

"Get out of town, boy," he said in an angry voice.

Eric didn't want them to think they had scared him off, so he explained, "I was leaving anyway on the day you arrested me. But I'm just going to sell the bags we've made and get more materials. As soon as I do, I'll be back."

The policeman fingered his gun belt. "We'll be waiting."

Chapter 3

"DON'T CALL ME MR. ERIC"

The old station wagon was rattling along at just under 30. Eric was anxious to get back to the loft, but since he had to drive through the center of town to get there from the tents he didn't want to give the police any excuse for stopping him.

He had been to New York where he had shown the first four bags to CORE and to every organization he could think of. He had asked them all to mail out notices about the bags and many had agreed to do so. But he had failed in his efforts to find a leather dealer who would give him credit. Now they had to wait until orders started coming in before they could get cash to purchase more materials.

Eric had managed to sell the bags in New York for $10 each, and he'd gotten a few orders paid for in advance, so he was able to buy some more leather. He had cut it and was just returning from delivering it to the women in the tents. They could fill the orders and keep a few dollars for their labor, but then they would be broke again and would have to wait for more money to come in.

Eric saw a sign showing he was in a 30 mile an hour zone and checked his speed. "Mustn't rush," he thought.

Then the police car appeared from nowhere and forced him to the curb. Eric had the familiar feeling of fear, cold and damp, come over him.

"You are under arrest," the policeman said with a smile.

"What for?"

"Speeding."

"But I was going under 30."

"The speed limit's 20."

"But the sign says 30."

"Tell it to the judge."

Eric did tell it to the judge, who didn't seem terribly interested in the facts and quickly sentenced him to 14 days in jail.

For two weeks Eric was kept all by himself. He refused to eat any of the food brought to him. Once in a while the police would beat him with a black jack, but most of the time he was left alone. When he was released, his fear stayed with him until he reached the black community and was safely inside his loft.

For the first time he realized how completely his outlook had changed. In the North a white person hurried nervously through a colored neighborhood until he reached the safety of a white area. Here it was just the opposite. Color had taken on a new meaning. A black person meant "friend," a white man, "enemy."

Soon after he got out of jail, Eric learned that the police had decided to limit his area of safety even more. If he stayed off the streets he would be left alone. They wouldn't raid the loft to get him. But if he set foot out of the loft he was certain to be arrested. So, as long as he was to remain in Brownsville, the huge ugly room with the old cot would be his entire world.

Eric had to learn to live within the four walls of the loft month after lonely month. He would give someone money and they would go to a restaurant and bring him back the 62-cent dinner. After a long while he bought a hot plate and a few pots and did his own cooking. He would go as far as the Negro grocery store a block away for supplies, and some of the families gave him whatever government food they felt they could spare. He wasn't drawing any salary, so he had to live off the few hundred dollars of his savings.

At night, Eric had only his books for company—and the police cars that prowled around the building at midnight with their alarms sounding, reminding him that there were worse places to be than his loft.

But Eric had a great deal of work to keep him busy. He had to do all the leather cutting for the bags. It was a long and difficult process, but since he was working for nothing he could keep labor costs down by doing it himself. And there was the business end to manage. Eric had no experience with book keeping, so he had to invent his own system. He had to learn about state sales taxes, federal taxes, licenses, purchasing, packing, insurance, and mailing.

Eric had to figure out how to put the little money they had to the best possible use. Although he wanted to build up extra money to buy materials, he felt it was most important to pay the ladies at a rate that was higher than the local wage scale. They each got $3.50 a bag. Since it took them between two to three hours to sew each bag, they were earning no less than $1.25 an hour. Eric wanted them to get a feeling that their time was worth something.

This was a very new idea. In Brownsville the going rate for a domestic servant was $9 a week. If an entire family worked full time in the fields, they would earn a total of $600 a year!

The idea Eric had the most trouble getting across to the women in the project was that they owned the business and that he was just an employee of theirs. At first he found it almost impossible to convince them that this was different from the usual case of the white man coming down to set up a factory and hiring cheap Negro labor. They would treat him like a white man and call him "Mr. Eric" or "Mr. Weinberger" and ask him what he wanted them to do. He would try to explain it to them over and over.

"This belongs to you. You are *my* boss. Any time you want to get rid of me you can fire me. I'm not making a cent. The money is yours. The Haywood Handicrafters League is yours. And please, don't call me Mr. Eric!"

But many of them still did not believe it. They had almost no education, so they couldn't check the books to see where the money was going. And they had learned the hard way never to trust a white man—even if he was an unusual one like Eric. As one of them once put it, "No matter how crazy he acts today, there's no telling what he'll do tomorrow."

But by the time Eric had been out of jail for two months, things were running well. Nine women, one from each tent and four from the shacks, were working in the project. Eric had mastered all the details of cutting, packing, and shipping and had found the necessary sources of supply. The group could turn out 70 bags a month. The orders would trickle in, and when there was enough money Eric would order leather for 70 more bags.

During this period, Eric heard that the Committee for Nonviolent Action was holding the South's first peace walk from Nashville to Washington, D.C. Eric wasn't expecting a new order of leather to arrive for a month, so he decided to take off a few days and join the march. At the end of the third day of the peace walk, Eric got a phone call from one of the leather workers who had somehow tracked him down. She was talking so fast Eric could hardly understand her.

"The money's just pouring in . . . We've got no leather . . . What are we going to do? There's all this money."

"Slow down," Eric said. "What money?"

"It's coming in the mail. Thousands of orders. It'll take years to catch up."

"Just how much money?"

"Well, we haven't counted it all, but there are over a thousand orders. That's . . . let's see . . . more than $10,000!"

Eric was surprised. No wonder the woman was excited. Then he realized what had happened. CORE must have included the notice about the bags in their national mailing to 40,000 people. Everyone received it on the same day and all the orders were coming in at once.

"That's great," he said.

"Maybe," the woman answered. "But please come on back and *do* something."

"Okay. I'm leaving right away. In the meantime, don't worry, and whatever you do, don't spend all that money."

Eric was only half kidding. When he returned he found the women sitting at the long tables in the loft surrounded by stacks of letters and checks, excited by their sudden good fortune, not knowing what to do about it.

First Eric had to explain that the money, over $10,000,

was not theirs to spend. They had to buy enough materials to make the bags and fill the orders. And now, at last, they would have enough extra money to buy leather in large quantities. They wouldn't have to wait months to save up enough for each new order.

In one day the Haywood Handicrafters League had become a financial success. And it had suddenly won respect in the black community. To fill the flood of orders, their group had grown to 72 members. There were some pretty big decisions to be made, but when the ladies turned to him for instructions, Eric insisted that the decisions be made by the members at a meeting.

The women may have been poor and not educated, but they knew how to run a meeting. They had become familiar with the principles of democracy through the traditions of the Baptist Church. A poor Negro church in the South couldn't afford a full time minister. A preacher would visit once a month, and the rest of the time the church was run by the members. So the ladies ran their business as they ran their church. Each meeting would begin with singing. Then the elected chairman would call the meeting to order. Plans were made, arguments were heard, and votes were taken. Some of the members were active and spoke out. Others were meek and they were put down for it.

At first, everyone went along with Eric's suggestions without argument. He had to keep reminding them that he was just "hired help" and, in fact, didn't even have a vote. Pretty soon the chairman got over the white-black problem and began treating Eric like a young snip who had to be put in his place once in a while. This pleased him very much. But he wasn't convinced that the plan of self help and self rule was really working— could it go on working if he wasn't there?

One day the whole idea was put to the test. They were way behind in filling their orders, so Eric rose at a meeting and made a suggestion he believed would help them catch up.

"When the leather comes in everybody gets the same number of bags to make. But some people are faster than others. When the quick ones are done they have to wait around for the slow ones to finish. Let's do it as a first come, first served idea and have everyone make bags as fast as they can."

Most of the women were against Eric's plan and they said so. "That's not fair. We should split the work up equally."

"Mrs. Johnson there is 70 years old and it takes her three weeks to do her share because she doesn't very often feel good enough to do any stitching."

"Old Mrs. Smith, she's got ten children and 20 grand children to look after. Mrs. Wilson hasn't got anything to do. Sure she would get them all done in a day and come back for more, but that's not fair."

"Right. She shouldn't get all the work and Mrs. Smith none."

A vote was taken and Eric's suggestion was defeated. At first he wasn't convinced, but he went along with their decision. Soon he realized that although they had been wrong in business terms, they had been absolutely right in community terms. Their way *was* fair and it worked. The League was no longer a crazy idea the strange white boy from the North was trying to explain and that they joined because it was better than starving. It had become a successful business which they took pride in owning and running.

Soon they were treating Eric like hired help. When his savings ran low they voted him a salary of $6 a week. When he had to go to New York on business, they would hotly debate whether they could afford to give him the $36 bus fare or if he should hitch hike. The vote could go either way.

Eric knew he was seeing the most magnificent thing about the dawning civil rights movement. The triumph of the movement couldn't be measured by how many people were registered to vote or even how many tote bags were sold. The true measure was the new spirit among people who had been told they were not as good as the whites for so long they had begun to believe it, people who really had never before held up their heads. For the first time they were taking charge of their own lives.

"Now," he thought with a smile, "they hardly ever call me Mr. Eric."

Chapter 4

MISSISSIPPI OR BUST

In August of 1962, Eric was invited to come to the slums of Chicago and teach non-violent methods to 40 college students at the summer non-violent training meeting of a small peace action group called Peace Makers. Eric met many interesting people but none so interesting—and attractive—as a young student named Elaine Makowski. They spent a great deal of time together and promised to see each other again.

By the spring of 1963, Eric had been in Brownsville for nearly a year and a half. The Haywood Handicrafters League had sold more than $30,000 worth of tote bags, over half of which had gone to its members.

In April, Eric went to New England to sell tote bags to college students. On April 23, he read about the murder of 35-year-old William Moore, the first civil rights death to get national notice in the papers. The southern born, white mailman from Baltimore had set out from Chattanooga, Tennessee, on a one man Freedom Walk. He had planned to deliver a letter, a plea for freedom for the Negroes, to the governor of Mississippi, Ross Barnett, at the state capitol in Jackson. He was wearing a sandwich-board sign which read, "Eat at Joe's, Both Black and White" and "Equal Rights for All —Mississippi or Bust." He had walked safely through a short stretch of Georgia, but soon after crossing into Alabama he was shot in the back at close range and left to die on U. S. Route 11. The word "Black" had been ripped from his sign.

A few days later, Eric got a call from Bob Gore, a civil rights leader he had met the year before.

"Have you got a spare sleeping bag I can borrow?" he asked Eric.

"What for?"

"CORE and SNCC are putting together a group to complete Moore's Freedom Walk."

"Not only do I have a sleeping bag, but I've got someone to go in it—me. I want to go along."

Eric had known at once that the walk was the right thing to do and he was the right person to do it. Rather than scaring him away, the dangers made it even more necessary that people experienced in the methods of nonviolence should go along. And he felt the walk had great meaning. The public had to become aware of what was happening in the South. The nation had found it too easy to close its eyes to violence. People refused to believe it could happen in their country. Now they had heard of William Moore, and Eric was determined they wouldn't forget.

On May 1, ten young men, five black and five white, set out from Chattanooga on the same route Moore had taken carrying signs like his. They walked the first few miles in Tennessee without trouble and then crossed into the north-east corner of Georgia. Before they would get to Alabama, and the spot where Moore had been shot, they had to travel 30 miles through Dade County, an area of Georgia with widely scattered small towns and long empty stretches of highway.

As the Freedom Marchers hiked along the side of the road, car loads of local young people drove past the line, moving to within inches of them and often forcing them to dive into ditches to keep from being run over. One car came close enough to Eric to hit the bag on his back. A crowd of whites followed the marchers the entire time, shouting and throwing eggs and rocks at them and once in a while firing shots. The only thing keeping them from attacking the marchers was a single state policeman walking ten feet behind the line of civil rights workers.

On the other side of the highway nearly 200 news men and camera men walked along with them, covering the event. Eric was surprised that the Freedom Walk was being given so much attention. The press, which later played such an important role in the movement by its stories of the struggle in the South, until recently had shown very little interest in civil rights. Now they were there in numbers, trying to get a close and honest look at what the ten young men were doing by walking with them and sharing their danger.

At the end of the day, local Negroes gave the marchers a fried chicken dinner and put them up for the night in their church. Even though they were afraid that the whites might attack their church, they felt they couldn't let the ten civil rights workers sleep on the road.

The Freedom Marchers attracted a big crowd in Georgia, and people came from all over the state to see them and to yell and throw things at them. They would stop their cars at the head of the line, get out, and form a group blocking the road. The ten men would have to walk through them, careful not to touch any of them. Eric knew if he even brushed against one of the group it would be used as an excuse to beat him up.

But, in spite of his fear, Eric found ways of reaching the people in the mob. After all, they were human beings and it was possible to talk to them. At noon the marchers took a break at the side of the highway. As they rested and ate the sandwiches brought to them by a local Negro women's church group, car loads of kids would come over a few at a time and stand and stare at the ten strange men they had been hearing about.

Then they made some remark like, "Hey, you nigger lovers, what are you doing down here?" Eric would answer their questions and explain what the Freedom Walk was all about. He knew that in addition to being tough and angry, the kids were also curious.

As Eric talked to them, they might come a little closer and ask more questions. Then Eric would ask them questions and pretty soon they would have a conversation going. Once in a while Eric would offer one of them half of his sandwich, and they would sit and eat and talk together. The kid would never be friendly. And Eric knew if he made one slip, said something that could be considered an insult, he would be beaten up. Many people had come over, wanting to kill him. When they left they did not agree with him, but they did, perhaps, understand him a little better.

By the time the Freedom Marchers reached the Alabama border on the third day, they were being followed by nearly a hundred screaming whites. Ahead of them they saw several dozen Alabama state policemen lined up just across the border, blocking their way. In a field next to the highway a huge crowd of whites had come to watch. Al Lingo, Alabama's commissioner of public safety, spoke to the marchers through a loud speaker.

"Halt! I order you to break up. If you take one step forward you will be arrested for disturbing the peace."

The ten young men waited until he had finished and then walked toward the waiting policemen. As the crowd cheered, the police charged the civil rights workers and began leading them roughly to the waiting patrol cars. Eric and two others went limp. The cops poked them with their three foot long electric cattle prods while the mob screamed with delight.

"Kill them! Stick them again!"

"Throw them niggers in the river!"

"Kill 'em! Kill 'em! Kill 'em!"

Eric was used to the cattle prods, so he just let his muscles jump. Finally the policemen gave up. They carried him to a police car and threw him in.

The Freedom Marchers were driven to the jail at Fort Payne, Alabama, not far from the spot where William Moore had fallen. Nine of them were led up the stairs and into the old brick building. Two state policemen had to carry Eric up the stairs. As they carried him through the door, a guard standing inside the entrance asked:

"What's the matter with him?"

"This one's a real trouble maker," one of the policemen replied.

Eric saw the guard smile. "Is that right?" he said. "Well, let's see if we can't do something about that."

Chapter 5

THE LONG FAST

Eric was thrown into a small cell with a cot taking up half the cramped space. On one side of the cell was a wall of bars facing a bull pen that held six tough looking prisoners. They were poor whites, between 18 and 25, who were in for stealing cars and fighting with the police. They seemed to know who Eric was and started picking on him as soon as he arrived. They would throw soda bottles at him and then duck back out of sight in case he threw them back. Whenever he tried to lie down on his cot, one of them would hit it through the bars with a long flat stick.

After a while, the white prisoners grew puzzled at why "the trouble maker" wasn't getting mad, throwing the bottles back, or complaining. They became curious, so

Eric sat on the edge of his bed, out of range of the stick, and talked to them.

"Who told you to come down here?" they asked.

"I don't do what I'm told. I do what I think is right."

They agreed that that was a good way to be, but they weren't sure he was telling the truth.

"I bet Bobby Kennedy sent you." Robert Kennedy was U. S. Attorney General at the time.

"The NAACP is probably paying you $1000 a day."

"Would you do this for $1000 a day?" Eric asked.

"Hell, no."

"Well," said Eric, "I wouldn't either." Then Eric asked them about themselves, about their problems. He decided that underneath, they weren't so bad.

"You don't get much out of the system, you know. In that sense you are not so different from the Negroes. You are both trying to get the same things."

One of them hit the bed with the stick, but Eric went right on.

"You think you are better off, but you don't have any land, tools, capital, or education. You think you have to keep the black man in his place. But he's not really your enemy. You are both victims of the system."

It became easy to talk to the prisoners. They were angry but not blind. They must have thought Eric was talking sense. From the tone of their voices, Eric had a feeling that it was safe for him to lie down. As he stretched out on the cot, one of the prisoners came over to the bars with a knife in his hand. Eric watched as he reached through the bars and stabbed down at his ankle.

Eric sensed that this was the test. He didn't move as the knife came down. The prisoner stopped with the point of the knife less than an inch from Eric's ankle. From then on, they were friends.

They invited Eric to join them in a game of cards. They sat close to the bars of his cell and played cards. They talked together like old friends. One of them said he was sorry for the way they had acted and said that the police had given them the knife and the stick.

When a guard saw them playing cards, he reported it to the sheriff, who was furious. This was not what he had in mind. So Eric was immediately moved to the large group cell where the other white Freedom Marchers were being kept. Shortly after he got there the five Negro civil rights workers were brought in. Eric was surprised, because all the jails in the South were segregated.

"What happened?" he asked.

"We had all the cats in the black section singing freedom songs," a Negro answered with a smile.

Eric was delighted. "Great. We've been here one day and already we've desegregated the Fort Payne jail!"

Eric found very little to do as the days dragged on. His thoughts became more and more centered around one idea—fasting, refusing to eat. As in the Brownsville jail, he couldn't bring himself to go along with the system by eating prison food. At first it was difficult and he was always hungry. But as the days became weeks, it got easier. The hunger was gone, and although he was growing weaker and weaker he had a sense of peace. There was the good feeling of being a free man.

After the Freedom Marchers had been in the Fort Payne jail for 16 days, the Alabama authorities decided to move them to Kilby, the state prison outside of Montgomery. CORE had been staging a sympathy demonstration outside the jail, and there was some talk that the Ku Klux Klan was planning to ride. It was feared they would take the ten prisoners out of jail and lynch them. So they were moved to Kilby, one of the South's worst prisons.

When they arrived, Eric, very weak, was dragged up a flight of stairs by his feet with his head hitting each step.

The civil rights workers had a large area to themselves and killed time by running around and playing games. They made a ball out of a towel knotted around a roll of toilet paper and used it to play basketball. Eric was too weak to join in, so he lay on his cot and read.

After Eric had spent five days in Kilby, the prison doctor became worried about his condition. He hadn't been drinking enough water and his body had become dehydrated—dried out. The doctor felt he might get seriously ill or even die. When he reported this, the prison warden said, "Let him die. It's his own fault." But the doctor insisted on treating Eric—in the prison hospital.

On the twenty-second day of his fast, Eric was dragged down the stairs and shoved in a wheel chair. He felt no pain, but he had almost no strength left in his body. As he was wheeled down the prison hall, the chair hit a bump and Eric fell out. Somehow the guards, rough a moment ago, were moved. They lifted him gently and put him carefully back in the chair.

Elaine, who was helping out in Brownsville during Eric's absence, came to visit him in the hospital. The warden had allowed her to see Eric in the hope that she would talk him out of fasting. But she understood and was in sympathy with what he was doing. "You never wrote me you were fasting," she told him, "but I had an idea you were. All your letters were about food—some great dinner you once had, our last meal together, and especially chocolate whipped cream pie."

Eric smiled. "Yes. I dream about it all the time."

After three days in the hospital, Eric was moved back to his cell. The guards carefully wheeled him down the hall and gently carried him up the same flight of stairs he had been dragged up by the feet when he had arrived eight days earlier. The guards also began having long conversations with the Freedom Marchers. Eric was too weak to talk long, so his friends did most of the talking.

By the time Eric's fast had gone on a full month, he had to lie on his cot all day. His cell mates were very worried about him. He didn't realize it, but he had turned into a skeleton. They knew that if he went without eating much longer, his body might suffer permanent damage. He also made them very nervous at meal times.

He wanted company, so he would sit with them and drink his cup of water while they ate. They all felt a sense of relief when after 15 days in Kilby prison, they were taken back to Fort Payne for trial.

The guards carried Eric down the stairs and over to his wheel chair. The assistant warden, who was happy to get rid of the ten Freedom Marchers, pushed the chair to the outside steps and tipped it over the edge. Eric tumbled down the long flight of stairs to the pavement below. A state policeman picked him up and threw him into a waiting patrol car where Eric passed out. As the policeman drove off, the other civil rights workers in the car explained that Eric hadn't eaten in 32 days. The policeman said he was sorry and made friendly conversation for the rest of the trip. It seemed fasting had the power to bring out the good in almost anybody.

On June 3, after spending the night in the Fort Payne jail, the ten Freedom Marchers were tried and found guilty. They were released on bail and appealed the case. Months later they won their appeal.

Many newspaper stories appeared about Eric's fast. They told of the 32 days without eating, the loss of 45 pounds. But the real meaning of Eric's fast was known only to himself, his fellow Freedom Marchers, and the handful of prison guards and prisoners who had come into brief touch with Eric and his courage.

Chapter 6

END OF THE ROAD

After his trial, Eric went to Atlanta with Elaine in order to recover. He went to work immediately on a very serious project—eating. Within the limits of his finances he tried to satisfy all the dreams about food he had had in prison. After 12 days of stuffing himself, he still felt weak. But when he heard that a group of civil rights workers were staging Atlanta's first non-violent demonstration—a sit-in at a segregated restaurant—he couldn't resist.

He joined the protest, was immediately arrested, and spent the next three days in a tiny cement cell with a light bulb burning 24 hours a day and empty except for a single army blanket. He refused to eat, but this time fasting really bothered him because he hadn't fully recovered from his 32-day fast.

A week after his release, Eric attended to a personal

matter he felt he had been putting off too long. He and Elaine went to Chattanooga, Tennessee, and got married. They moved to Brownsville, in the loft over the store.

Together they ran the tote bag project and managed to live on Eric's small salary. Even at a dollar a day, they were doing better than most of Brownsville's Negroes. And they weren't starving. When they received a check for $10 as a wedding present, they decided to spend it all on milk shakes. Every day for a month they each had an extra thick one, southern style.

That summer Brownsville's Negro community was getting caught up in the new spirit of the civil rights movement that was sweeping the South. The high school kids had a case of "demonstration fever," which had spread from Birmingham, Alabama. Eric was asked if he knew anything about such things. He was happy to help.

Eric ran training courses in nonviolence for the kids and organized the protest. In the middle of August, Eric and 12 young Negroes marched to the Brownsville court house carrying signs demanding freedom and equal rights. The whites were waiting for them.

The police met the marchers with dogs, fire hoses, and tear gas, while a mob armed with guns and clubs cried for blood. The police directed most of their fury at Eric. He was badly beaten and was burned by a chemical that a policeman sprayed on him while he lay helpless on the ground.

Eric was arrested and dragged to the jail. One side of his face and body was so badly burned that he had to remove his clothes and could neither stand or lie down. He spent his first day in jail crawling around his cell on his hands and knees. Local whites brought in groups of Sunday school children to look at him. They laughed at the sight of the naked prisoner, his face covered with purple scabs, the flesh peeling off his flaming red body.

After three days, a lawyer got Eric out of jail and into a Memphis hospital, where he spent a week being treated for his burns.

In September, almost two years after Eric had arrived, he and Elaine decided to leave Brownsville. There were many reasons for their decision. The sheriff had told Eric's lawyer that if the civil rights worker didn't leave the county, he would be charged with attacking a police officer during his recent arrest. There were plenty of police who would act as "witnesses," and the sheriff felt certain he could get a conviction and lock Eric up for three years.

Eric might have stayed and fought the case, but he discovered that since the demonstration, certain middle-class leaders in the black community no longer considered him welcome. They were afraid they would lose what little power they had in Brownsville if the young people held more demonstrations.

Eric was sorry to leave the Haywood Handicrafters League. He had become very close to many of the members and their families. Strong bonds of friendship had grown between them. The experiment had worked. It had brought in much more money than he had expected. Even so, that wasn't the project's major achievement. Most important, it had proved to the Negroes that they could help themselves. It had given them a feeling of pride and personal worth that couldn't be measured in dollars and cents. But to be truly successful, the league had to carry on without outside help.

Eric and Elaine spent the winter of 1963–64 on a speaking tour of New England colleges raising money for a leather sandal-making project they wanted to start in Mississippi. In March, after they had raised a few hundred dollars, they moved to Canton, Mississippi, and tried to set up as Eric had in Brownsville. But Mississippi was not Tennessee. When Eric tried to get the licenses he needed, the authorities laughed in his face. And the black community wasn't ready to get involved in such a project. Eric and Elaine found themselves without a job.

But they weren't idle for long. CORE was trying to organize a movement in Canton, so they joined the task force as "junior staff members." Actually, at $15 a week they felt quite rich compared to their Brownsville days. In Canton Eric met a remarkable civil rights worker named James Chaney. The 21-year-old Negro from Meridian, Mississippi, plunged without fear into the most backward areas to organize extremely poor Negroes. He had often been chased through the streets by members of the Klan armed with rifles.

In June 1964, the civil rights movement mounted a major attack on Mississippi. The leading groups joined forces with thousands of northern college students who were planning to spend their summer vacation doing civil rights work in the state. Various projects throughout Mississippi sent representatives up to Oxford, Ohio, to train the students.

Eric and Elaine went up from Canton. They stopped at Meridian on the way and picked up Chaney and a fellow CORE member, Michael Schwerner. Schwerner, a 24-year-old New Yorker, had run an active community center and led a very successful drive to get people to register to vote. He had a reputation for being the best white civil rights worker in the South. In the eyes of Meridian's whites he was also the most hated.

The four drove up to Oxford together and began to work with the first batch of 40 students. Toward the end of the first group's training meetings, Eric and Michael Schwerner discussed the new people and tried to decide who would go to Canton with Eric and who would go with Michael back to Meridian. They agreed that the most promising student was 20-year-old Andrew Goodman from New York. He was able, sensible, and aware of the danger without being frightened. Andy felt more could be accomplished in Meridian, so he chose to go with Michael Schwerner.

On June 21, a few days before the first training meeting was over, Michael heard that a Negro church had been burned in Philadelphia, Mississippi, a small town near Meridian. He felt he had to go there immediately to see what he could do to help. James Chaney knew the area well and decided to go with him. Andy Goodman wanted to go, too, and start working with Michael right away. The three young men left that afternoon.

The next day the people in Oxford heard stories that Schwerner, Chaney, and Goodman had disappeared. The northern press wasn't alarmed, and the Mississippi press said they were hiding out to give the state a bad name. But civil rights leaders at Oxford took it very seriously. They assumed the worst.

Since the police and FBI weren't doing anything, SNCC organized an investigating team and Eric asked to be a part of it. The leaders felt it was too dangerous for any whites to go along, but Eric insisted. He realized that he was risking being killed, but he felt personally involved with the three young men. He had to go.

Two days later the investigating team was at the air port ready to leave for Mississippi when they heard that a burned station wagon had been found. Police had said it was the car the three civil rights workers had last been seen in. Now it was clear to everybody that the three were dead. The FBI went to work on the case, and Eric's investigating team never left Oxford.

The students at the training meetings were shaken by the event, but they had been told from the start that there might be a hundred deaths before the summer was

141

over. And there might have been, if the three murders hadn't become a major news story throughout the world.

No whites and only a few Negroes were killed in the months that followed. The deaths of Schwerner, Chaney, and Goodman not only brought the civil rights movement to the attention of the nation and the federal government, but probably saved the lives of many other young students during the Mississippi Summer Project.

In September, Eric and Elaine tried to take the place of Michael Schwerner and run the Meridian Community Center. For seven months they struggled, but without much success. Eric realized that a change was taking place in the movement.

The black leaders were beginning to ask why whites should run a Negro Community Center. They didn't feel whites should be deeply involved. Local Negroes should carry the burden of the struggle for equal rights.

It made good sense to Eric, although there was still much he wanted to do to help. He had become a part of the struggle when it had barely begun. He had seen it grow and had helped it develop. It was difficult for him to accept the fact that his part in it would have to end. But if one of his goals had been to help southern Negroes take charge of their lives, then he was bound to be one of the victims of his own success.

If "Tent City" was the starting point of Eric's part in the Freedom Movement, then "Bloody Sunday" marked its end. On March 7, 1965, more than 500

Negroes involved in the Selma, Alabama, drive to get people to register to vote set out on a march to the state capitol in Montgomery to demand their right to register. As they marched out of Selma, state police and men on horseback charged the Negroes and beat them to the ground, seriously injuring 84. Martin Luther King, Jr., who had organized the march, sent out a call for everyone in the movement to come to Selma and help complete the Freedom March.

Thousands of people of every age came from all over the nation. Eric and Elaine rushed to Selma to take their places with the other marchers. It meant a great deal to Eric to be there. He knew it would probably be the last big civil rights demonstration he would ever be a part of, and perhaps the last one of its kind for the movement. The Negro leaders had decided that everyone could march out of Selma, but that only a few important white people could march the whole way to Montgomery. The rest would return to Selma and wait there until the marchers reached the edge of the capital. Then the white marchers in Selma would drive out and join the main body as it entered Montgomery.

Eric wanted to walk the whole way, but he knew that the Negroes had good reasons for their plan. They wanted to leave off workers in all the black communities along the way. It was important to them that the local Negroes see a black march, one they could identify with, one they could trust. Though he understood the reason, Eric was deeply disappointed.

Eric and Elaine walked out of Selma with the Freedom March. When they got out into the country, they and hundreds of other white marchers had to return to Selma and wait. Eric tried to make himself useful as the days passed, but there was little he could do. There were many people working on the running of the march. Eric just didn't fit in. He was not an organization man. He had always played an individual role in the movement. Now, it seemed, those days were over for him.

On March 25, as Eric finally entered Montgomery with Elaine at his side and hundreds of blacks and whites around him, he knew that this might be the end of one great adventure, but that another one, perhaps even greater, lay just ahead. He had been offered a job at the New York office of the Committee for Nonviolent Action, playing an important role in the growing movement against war. He knew he would be more useful there than he could be in the South.

The struggle for peace would not be understood by many people, and it would be as difficult and possibly as dangerous as the struggle for equal rights. But as long as Eric could follow his belief in nonviolence and help build a better society, no risk would be too great.